ckman

Fast Forward Writing

LEVEL **5** to LEVEL **6**

Hodder & Stoughton

A MEMBER OF THE HODDER HEADLINE GROUP

Acknowledgements

The author and publisher would like to thank the following for:

Copyright text:

pp1, 3 and 6 *Saffy's Angel* © Hilary McKay, 2001, Hodder Children's Books. Reproduced by permission of Hodder and Stoughton Limited; pp4, 5, 7 and 8 *Pharos* © Alice Thompson, 2002, Virago; pp10 and 11 Extracts from *Hydra* by Robert Swindells, published by Corgi. Reprinted by permission of the Random House Group Ltd; pp13, 14 and 16 *Stormbreaker* © Anthony Horowitz, 2000, Walker Books Ltd. Reproduced by permission of Walker Books Ltd, London SE11 5HJ; p21 Quotes from *Writers on Writing* © Ed. Jon Winokur, 1986, Hodder Headline; p22 'Paradise Regained' © Natasha Polyviou in *Time Out*, 11 February 2004; p23 *Delia Smith's Summer Collection* © Delia Smith, 1993, BBC Books. Reproduced with the permission of BBC Worldwide Limited; pp33, 34, 35 and 36 *POW* © Martin Booth, 2000, Puffin. Reproduced by permission of Penguin Books Ltd; pp37 and 42 Extracts from *Immediate Action* by Andy McNab, published by Corgi. Reprinted by permission of the Random House Group Ltd; pp38 and 39 *The First Men in the Moon* by H.G. Wells, 1901, first serialised in *Cosmopolitan*; p39 *The Rainbow* by D.H. Lawrence, 1915, Penguin; p39 *The Old Wives' Tale* by Arnold Bennett, 1908, Penguin; pp40 and 42 'Shooting an Elephant' from *Inside the Whale* © George Orwell, 1936, Penguin. Reproduced by permission of Bill Hamilton as the Literary Executor of the Estate of the late Sonia Brownell Orwell and Secker & Warburg Ltd; p41 *A Kestrel for a Knave* © Barry Hines, 1968, Penguin. Reproduced by permission of Penguin Books Ltd; p54 Claire Southern of *Rough Guide*; p58 'Death at a public fight' © Vickie Chachere in *Associated Press* from polkonline.com. Reprinted with permission of The Associated Press; p62 'The Stolen Cigar Case', *Faber Book of Parodies* © Bret Harte, 1984, Faber & Faber; pp64 and 65 *Three Men in a Boat* by Jerome K. Jerome, 1889, Penguin; p67 'Politics and the English Language' from *Inside the Whale* © George Orwell, 1946, Penguin. Reproduced by permission of Bill Hamilton as the Literary Executor of the Estate of the late Sonia Brownell Orwell and Secker & Warburg Ltd; p68 'Letter to a Newly-Married Lady' by Mrs Chapone, from the Eighteenth Century; p75 *How are Verses Made?* © Vladimir Mayakovsky, 1926, Bristol Classical Press; pp76 and 78 *Macbeth* by William Shakespeare, 1606; p78 'Lamia' by John Keats, 1820; p83 'The Arc of Joan' © Al Alvarez in the *Observer*, 8 February 2004; p85 *The BMA Family Health Encyclopaedia* © Ed. Tony Smith, 1990, Dorling Kindersley. Reproduced by permission of Dorling Kindersley Ltd; p89 'Beckham's Hotshots' © Barry Davies in the *Observer*, 22 February 2004; p90 'Random drugs tests for pupils' © Gaby Hinsliff in the *Observer*, 22 February 2004; p100 and 102 *The Idea of Perfection* © Kate Grenville, 1999, Picador; p106 *Don't Look Now* © Daphne du Maurier, 1971, Penguin; p108 *The Breakthrough* © Daphne du Maurier, 1971, Penguin; pp109 and 112 *The Road to Wigan Pier* © George Orwell, 1936, Penguin. Reproduced by permission of Bill Hamilton as the Literary Executor of the Estate of the late Sonia Brownell Orwell and Secker & Warburg Ltd; pp112 and 113 *Mini Sagas* 1999 © Telegraph Group Limited and contributors; p114 *Homage to Catalonia* © George Orwell, 1937, Penguin. Reproduced by permission of Bill Hamilton as the Literary Executor of the Estate of the late Sonia Brownell Orwell and Secker & Warburg Ltd.

Acknowledgements for copyright photographs and images continued on the inside back cover.

Orders: please contact Bookpoint Ltd, 130 Milton Park, Abingdon, Oxon, OX14 4SB.
Telephone: (44) 01235 827720, Fax: (44) 01235 400454.
Lines are open from 9.00am – 6.00pm, Monday to Saturday, with a 24 hour message answering service.
You can also order through our website: www.hodderheadline.co.uk

British Library Cataloguing in Publication Data
A catalogue record for this title is available from The British Library

ISBN 0 340 88346 4

First published 2004
Impression number   10 9 8 7 6 5 4 3 2 1
Year   2010 2009 2008 2007 2006 2005 2004

Copyright © 2004 Sue Hackman

Cover artwork by Neil Leslie, Début Art.
Typeset by Lorraine Inglis Design.
Printed in Italy for Hodder & Stoughton Educational, a division of Hodder Headline, 338 Euston Road, London NW1 3BH.

Contents

A. *Ways of telling*

Aims of this unit of work

- To develop a strong, effective narrative voice
- To increase the repertoire of narrative techniques
- To develop versatile narrative writing skills

Objectives addressed (by year)

Year 7 objectives

Sn7	Speech punctuation
Sn15	Vary formality
R6	Active reading
Wr6	Characterisation
Wr7	Narrative devices
Wr14	Evocative description

Year 8 objectives

Sn2	Variety of sentence structure
Sn6	Grouping sentences
R10	Development of key ideas
Wr1	Effective planning
Wr5	Narrative commentary

Year 9 objectives

Sn4	Integrate speech, reference and quotation
Wr1	Review own writing
Wr5	Narrative techniques
Wr11	Descriptive detail

Delivery

The unit is organised in four masterclasses of around 2 hours each for use by individuals or small groups working co-operatively:

Masterclass 1: Using speech and dialogue
Masterclass 2: Switching between narrative approaches
Masterclass 3: Seeing the story
Masterclass 4: Establishing a voice

Total: 8 hours

B. *Improving expression*

Aims of this unit of work

- To sharpen vocabulary choices
- To develop more sophisticated sentence structures
- To improve early drafting processes

Objectives addressed (by year)

Year 7 objectives

Wd14	Word meaning in context
Wd16	Unfamiliar words
Wd21	Subject vocabulary
Sn1	Subordinate clauses
Sn2	Noun phrases
Sn12	Sequencing paragraphs
R7	Identify main ideas
R15	Endings
Wr1	Drafting process
Wr2	Planning formats
Wr5	Story structure
Wr10	Organise texts appropriately

Year 8 objectives

Wd7b	Unfamiliar words
Wd9	Specialist vocabulary
Sn1	Complex sentences
Sn2	Variety of sentence structure
Sn6	Grouping sentences
R5	Trace developments
R10	Development of key ideas
Wr1	Effective planning
Wr10	Effective information

Year 9 objectives

Wd7	Layers of meaning
Sn1	Complex sentences
Sn6	Paragraph organisation
Wr1	Review own writing
Wr5	Narrative techniques

Delivery

The unit is organised in four masterclasses of around 2 hours each for use by individuals or small groups working co-operatively:

Masterclass 5: Managing vocabulary
Masterclass 6: Getting more from your words
Masterclass 7: Extending your sentences
Masterclass 8: Developing your ideas

Total: 8 hours

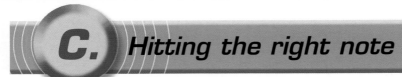

C. *Hitting the right note*

Aims of this unit of work

- To increase the repertoire of writing registers
- To develop a confident, plain, standard writing style
- To develop control of vocabulary, expression and tone

Objectives addressed (by year)

Year 7 objectives

Sn15	Vary formality
Sn16	Speech and writing
Sn17	Standard English
Wr10	Organise texts appropriately
Wr15	Express a view
Wr18	Present findings

Year 8 objectives

Wd12	Formality and word choice
Sn10	Informal to formal
Sn11	Standard English and dialect
Sn12	Degrees of formality
Wr7	Establish the tone
Wr8	Experiment with conventions
Wr15	Advice about options
Wr16	Balanced analysis

Year 9 objectives

Sn3	Degrees of formality
Sn7	Exploit conventions
Sn9	Sustained standard English
Wr15	Impartial guidance
Wr16	Balanced analysis

Delivery

The unit is organised in four masterclasses of around 2 hours each for use by individuals or small groups working co-operatively:

Masterclass 9: The assertive voice
Masterclass 10: The discursive voice
Masterclass 11: Using humour
Masterclass 12: The formal voice

Total: 8 hours

D. *Handling text*

Aims of this unit of work

- To improve the use of writing for different purposes
- To manipulate, tailor and organise text to clarify its meaning
- To gain greater control over the structure of writing

Objectives addressed (by year)

Year 7 objectives

Wd20	Connectives
Sn9	Main point of paragraph
Sn10	Paragraph structure
Sn12	Sequencing paragraphs
Sn13f	Discursive writing
Sn15	Vary formality
Sn17	Standard English
R3	Compare presentation
R4	Note-making
R10	Media audiences
Wr1	Drafting process
Wr2	Planning formats
Wr3	Exploratory writing
Wr10	Organise texts appropriately

Year 8 objectives

Wd10	Prepositions and connectives
Wd12	Formality and word choice
Sn7	Cohesion and coherence
Sn9	Adapting text types
Sn10	Informal to formal
Sn12	Degrees of formality
R1	Combine information
R3	Note-making formats
R8	Transposition
Wr1	Effective planning
Wr2	Anticipate reader reaction
Wr3	Writing to reflect
Wr7	Establish the tone
Wr10	Effective information
Wr15	Advice about options
Wr16	Balanced analysis

Year 9 objectives

Wd8	Connectives for developing thought
Sn3	Degrees of formality
Sn9	Sustained standard English
R2	Synthesise information
R3	Note-making at speed
Wr1	Review own writing
Wr9	Integrate information
Wr10	Explain connections
Wr16	Balanced analysis

Delivery

The unit is organised in four masterclasses of around 2 hours each for use by individuals or small groups working co-operatively:

Masterclass 13: Responding in writing
Masterclass 14: Making comparisons
Masterclass 15: Tailoring text
Masterclass 16: Synthesising text

Total: 8 hours

E. *Writing for the test*

Aims of this unit of work

- To develop the skills of analytic, critical writing
- To write more effectively in examination conditions
- To develop mental formulation strategies for sentence, paragraph and text level

Objectives addressed (by year)

Year 7 objectives

Sn14	Subject conventions
R2	Extract information
R4	Note-making
R7	Identify main ideas
R8	Infer and deduce
R12	Character, setting and mood
R14	Language choices
Wr19	Reflective writing

Year 8 objectives

R1	Combine information
R3	Note-making formats
R4	Versatile reading
R7	Implied and explicit meaning
R10	Development of key ideas
Wr1	Effective planning
Wr17	Integrate evidence
Wr18	Critical review

Year 9 objectives

Sn4	Integrate speech, reference and quotation
Sn5	Shape paragraphs rapidly
R3	Note-making at speed
R5	Evaluate own critical writing
R12	Rhetorical devices
Wr1	Review own writing
Wr3	Formal essay
Wr16	Balanced analysis
Wr17	Cite textual evidence

Delivery

The unit is organised in four masterclasses of around 2 hours each for use by individuals or small groups working co-operatively:

Masterclass 17: Critical tools
Masterclass 18: Quoting and referring
Masterclass 19: Explaining effects
Masterclass 20: Answers to big questions

Total: 8 hours

1. Using speech and dialogue

In this masterclass you will learn how to:

- punctuate speech
- make effective use of the 'speech tag'
- choose when to use dialogue.

How to punctuate speech

There are only a handful of rules about speech. Find a page or two of dialogue in a novel and use it to work out the rules.

Activity

1 Complete the sentences:

Rules of speech punctuation

> **1** Put speech marks around…
> **2** Put commas between…
> **3** If the speech goes on uninterrupted into a second paragraph, then leave out…
> **4** The comma is always positioned before…
> **5** Follow a speech mark with a capital letter only if…
> **6** Only one person may speak in any…
> **7** If someone new starts to speak, you must…
> **8** If the speech ends in a ? or a !…

2 Punctuate this dialogue:

Driving lesson 1

The driving instructor said to Caddy Now Cadmium, we are coming up to a crossroads. I should like you to take the turn on the right. Right said Caddy, happily, very pleased to be out with Michael again. I'll remember! You should be slowing down. Look in your mirror. Caddy looked and said I don't like this lipstick.

From *Saffy's Angel* by Hilary McKay

Check your answers at the end of this masterclass.

Making effective use of the speech tag

The speech tag is the part of the sentence that tells you about the speaker. For example: he said, she cried, we shouted.

Activity

Get into groups of three or four to come up with as many words as possible to use instead of *said*. You have five minutes.

Strengthening the verb

You can add an *–ly* adverb to the speech tag to suggest how the speech was made. For example:

...she said **quietly**
...she whispered **archly**

or you can use a phrase:

...she said **in an even voice**
...she declared **with passion in her voice and her eyes flashing**

but you can also keep it short and powerful by choosing a strong verb:

...she **spat**
...she **mewed**

Leaving out the speech tag

You can leave out the speech tag if you want the reader to work harder at who says what and if there are other ways of making it clear who is speaking.

Activity

How do you know who is speaking the underlined speech?

Driving lesson 2

'I can't believe you just did that,' said Michael.

'That was very, very brave,' agreed Rose, unclamping her fingers from the edge of the seat. 'Zipping in front of that enormous lorry. I'm sorry I screamed.'

'Perfectly natural reaction,' said Michael. 'Have you seen those cyclists ahead, Caddy?'

'No. Oh yes. Sorry. Shut my eyes for a moment.'

'Can you drive with your eyes shut?' enquired Rose.

'No. No, I can't. Missed. Good.'

'Missed what?'

'The cyclists.'

Michael put a hand on the steering wheel and said Caddy should take the next turn on the left and then pull up and park. Caddy pulled into a bus stop and thirteen people waved her away. Rose waved back.

From *Saffy's Angel* by Hilary McKay

Activity

- List the clues that let the reader know who is speaking.

Choosing when to use dialogue

The alternatives to using dialogue are:

1   Reporting instead of quoting what was said. For example:

Cameron told Simon to dig up the vegetables.

2   Leaving it out altogether. For example:

Simon dug up the vegetables.

Use dialogue when:

● the actual words spoken are important
● the dialogue moves the plot along.

There is no dialogue in this passage, though talk is going on:

Above in the lantern room, Cameron looked out to sea. There was going to be another bad storm soon. He told Simon to dig up as many vegetables from the garden as possible, as soon they were going to be ruined by sea spray. They locked the doors and windows and waited. The afternoon was unnaturally dark and eerily windless. During supper the others were joking and laughing in a way Lucia had never seen before. It was contagious and she was soon joining in with their pre-storm hysteria, which gave her a sense of warmth and belonging.

From *Pharos* by Alice Thompson

Activity

Why might the writer have chosen to report the talk rather than give the dialogue?

Mixing dialogue and narrative

Study this extract, which mixes dialogue and narrative:

'What are you doing here?' he asked.

'I heard laughter. A child's laughter.'

His immobile face didn't flinch. He simply looked at her a second longer than was natural.

'It will be the wailing the reef makes. The reef is in a hollow cavern. Sometimes the waves, as they rush in, compress the air and force it out, making a howling cry.'

'But this was laughter.'

She felt angry, his tone was patronising, implying that she was conceiving fancies in her head. Also, the laughter had unnerved her and she tried to calm herself. But she felt a sudden, irrational, violent urge to push Cameron down the steps. He looked precariously balanced there.

'Laughter can sometimes sound like crying,' he said. 'Go back to bed.'

From *Pharos* by Alice Thompson

Activity

- Find two places where the writer has cut away from the dialogue and put in narrative.
- In pairs, read aloud the dialogue like a play, leaving out the speech tags and narrative.
- Discuss what is lost when you do this.
- Discuss what is added by each of the narrative paragraphs.
- Why did the writer choose narrative in these two places rather than having the characters speaking their minds?

Hot Tip ▶▶

Writers often cut away from dialogue to:

- reveal the inner thoughts and feelings of the characters
- 'see' how characters react
- signal a pause in the conversation
- tell you about other things that happen as they speak.

 **Test it**

Your test task is to reread the extract on page 4. Four characters are sitting around a table in a lighthouse. Suddenly, the storm breaks and begins to rage. The sea becomes wild. Write 20 lines starting with the first clap of thunder, using dialogue and commentary to show how quickly their hilarity turns to worry and then turns to fear.

What you get marks for

Putting speech marks in the right places	1 mark
Putting commas in the right places	1 mark
Putting capital letters in the right places	1 mark
Having only one person speaking in a paragraph	1 mark
Choosing effective speech tags	2 marks
Making effective use of narrative between the dialogue	4 marks
Total	**10 marks**

ANSWERS

Rules of speech

1 Put speech marks around the spoken words.
2 Put commas between the spoken words and the rest of the sentence.
3 If the speech goes on uninterrupted into a second paragraph, then leave out the speech mark at the end of the first paragraph.
4 The comma is always positioned before the speech marks.
5 Follow a speech mark with a capital letter only if it is the start of a normal sentence.
6 Only one person may speak in any paragraph.
7 If someone new starts to speak, you must start a new paragraph.
8 If the speech ends in a ? or a !, no need for a comma there.

Driving lesson 1

The driving instructor said to Caddy, 'Now Cadmium, we are coming up to a crossroads. I should like you to take the turn on the right.'

'Right,' said Caddy, happily, very pleased to be out with Michael again. 'I'll remember!'

'You should be slowing down. Look in your mirror.'

Caddy looked and said, 'I don't like this lipstick.'

2. Switching between narrative approaches

In this masterclass you will learn how to:

- switch between action, description, quotation, inner reflection and comment as appropriate
- decide which is the best each time
- make more use of description and reflection.

Different narrative approaches

There are five basic elements in a narrative. Writers shift between them, even within a paragraph.

1 Action

2 Description

3 Quotation (such as dialogue or a letter)

4 Inner reflection (what the characters are thinking and feeling)

5 Comment (when the narrator comments on events)

The trick is to choose the best approach, and know when to shift between them.

> Just then she heard footsteps and flung round to see Cameron standing on the final step, looking at her. In the bright light of the lamp and mirrors his face looked like a death mask. 'What are you doing here?' he asked.

From *Pharos* by Alice Thompson

Activity

Read the extract and say which of the five approaches is being used in each sentence.

Shifting between approaches

Identify the narrative approaches taken in each of the disguised parts of the following extract:

She slowly walked towards the door that Charlotte had forbidden her to open. She put her hand on the handle and turned it. The door opened easily and silently. Ινσιδε ωασ α ωινδοωλεσσ ροομ. Τηερε ωασ α χηαιν ατταχηεδ το τηε ωαλλ ανδ α χηαιν νεξτ το τηε βεδ. Δυστ χοϖερεδ αλλ τηε συρφαχεσ. Ιτ σμελτ λικε α μαυσολευμ.

Iron instruments lay by the basin. Knives and forceps. Soiled napkins were piled up in a bucket. On closer examination of the unmade bed she saw the sheets were rust–stained with dried blood.

Closing the door of the dark ominous place, Lucia ran to her room. She had to escape from the island. Tearing a page from her book of false memories she wrote:

Πλεασε χονταχτ τηε ΔΣ οφ τηε Νορτηερν Λιγητηουσε Βοαρδ. Ι αμ στρανδεδ ον ϑαχοβ σ Ροχκ. Πλεασε χομε ανδ ρεσχυε με. Τηερε ισ δαρκνεσσ ηερε.

She rolled the note into a cylinder and pushed it into the neck of an old cologne bottle she had found washed up on the beach. She threw the bottle with all her strength out of her window and watched it float away on the outgoing tide. Τηερε ωασ λιττλε ηοπε, σηε τηουγητ, οφ ανψονε φινδινγ ιτ, οφ ανψονε υνδερστανδινγ ωηερε σηε ωασ. Βυτ ατ λεαστ ιτ γαϖε ηερ σομε κινδ οφ ηοπε.

From *Pharos* by Alice Thompson

Activity

1   What approach do you expect to find in the disguised sentences?

2   Discuss the clues that suggested this to you.

3   Check your answers at the end of this masterclass.

4   Write what you think would 'work' in the disguised sentences.

5   Compare your ideas with the writer's original version at the end of this masterclass.

Hot Tip ▶▶

Action is over-used. Keep it down. Avoid 'and then…and then…and then…' Break it up and give it deeper meaning by interspersing it with reflection.

Dialogue is over-used, too. Use it sparingly, when the spoken words matter.

Description is good for picturing things when their appearance is important. Details make it sound authentic. Readers who enjoy visualising the story enjoy description.

Inner reflection adds depth and feeling to stories, and is the most under-used element. It makes the reader care for your characters.

Narrative commentary is good if you want the narrator to be a character, too. You must be able to handle the confident voice.

Clunky plots and flat characters can be improved by adding in description and reflection.

Using description

Description helps the reader see what is in the writer's mind, yet you do not have to write a complete description. A telling detail is a quick way of creating an impression.

Look how the writer switches between action and description in this extract:

> He glanced to his left. The High Street stood deserted, bathed in amber light. He looked right, to where the streetlamps stopped and the High Street became the Warminster Road. Nothing moved upon it. The only sound was the soft rustle of beech leaves in the breeze.
>
> He looked across, into the black mouth of the shelter. She was there, a pale shape sitting on the bench, watching him with her Mona Lisa eyes. A familiar ache rose in his chest and he swallowed hard as he crossed the road.
>
> 'Hi. How long have you been here?'

From *Hydra* by Robert Swindells

Activity

1 The writer chose to switch between description and action. What is he suggesting?

2 Notice that the last sentence is neither description nor action – what is it?

3 Write a new paragraph in the same style to go just before the two above, describing the man as he approaches the High Street through dark back alleys.

Three common and very useful techniques are used here:

- ending with a sentence that is different from the rest
- setting up a pattern of sentences that shifts between action and description
- using an approach that reflects what is happening.

Using reflection

Reflection takes us inside the thoughts and feelings of the characters. Time stops whilst we listen in to them. Reflection is good for:

- building up sympathy for characters
- understanding motivation
- understanding how events affect a character
- making the story more realistic
- slowing down events so that the reader can take them in.

Find the three reflective sentences in this extract:

> They walked back along the hedge and crawled through. It was very dark. Ben peered into the field. 'I'm sure it's just about here.'
>
> 'D'you bring a torch?' Midge murmured.
>
> Ben felt a stab of anger and self-contempt. Damn. No watch, no guts and now no torch. What a fantastic impression he must be making on her. He shook his head, dumbly.
>
> ''S OK – I have.'

From *Hydra* by Robert Swindells

Activity

1   Reread the extract, leaving out the reflective sentences. What is lost?

2   The writer makes you see events from Ben's point of view. One reason for this is that you are allowed inside his head to hear his thoughts and feelings. Find two other ways in which the writer makes you see the events from Ben's point of view.

3   Change the three reflective sentences to suggest completely different feelings inside Ben. Do any other words in the extract have to be changed to fit with your new Ben?

Test it

Your test task is to write five or six paragraphs entitled **Night Patrol** in which your main character is a security guard or soldier patrolling on night watch. He or she is suddenly alerted by a suspicious sound. Follow your character as he or she investigates the source of the sound. Switch between action and description. Introduce inner reflection and maybe dialogue, as fits the story.

What you get marks for

Switching between action and description	3 marks
Using reflection to give an insight into the character's thoughts and feelings	3 marks
Mixing narrative approaches that fit what is going on	4 marks
Total	**10 marks**

ANSWERS

Disguised paragraphs

1 – Description

2 – Quotation

3 – Reflection

Writer's originals

1 The door opened easily and silently. Inside was a windowless room. There was a chain attached to the wall and a chain next to the bed. Dust covered all the surfaces. It smelt like a mausoleum.

2 Please contact the DS of the Northern Lighthouse Board. I am stranded on Jacob's Rock. Please come and rescue me. There is darkness here.

3 There was little hope, she thought, of anyone finding it, of anyone understanding where she was. But at least it gave her some kind of hope.

3. Seeing the story

In this masterclass you will learn how to:

- help your reader to visualise a scene
- position your reader to see events as you want them seen
- help the reader's imagination.

Visualising

You can help your reader to see things better if you:

- offer striking details that capture the whole
- give visual hints such as colours, shades and shapes
- build up associations by using simile, metaphor or suggestive names
- emphasise or repeat distinguishing features.

Notice how these are used here:

Alex shivered. There was something about the new arrival that made his skin crawl.

And yet the man was ordinary to look at. Grey suit, grey hair, grey lips and grey eyes. His face was expressionless, the eyes behind the square, gunmetal spectacles completely empty. Perhaps that was what disturbed Alex. Whoever this man was, he seemed to have less life than anyone in the cemetery. Above or below ground.

Someone tapped Alex on the shoulder and he turned round to see Mr Crawley leaning over him. 'That's Mr Blunt.'

From *Stormbreaker* by Anthony Horowitz

Activity

1 Find an example of each technique in the extract.

2 Write a single paragraph portrait of a stranger using the four techniques above.

Positioning the reader

There are several ways of putting the reader where you want them to be:

- Tell them where they are.
- Decide where they are standing and show only what can be seen from there.
- Influence their point of view by loading the language.

Notice the picture that appears in your mind as you read this:

Parachute drop from an airplane

There was a loud buzz and the red light turned green. The assistant pilot had climbed through from the cockpit. He reached for a handle and pulled open a door set in the back of the aircraft, allowing the cold air to rush in. Alex could see a single square of night. It was raining. The rain howled past.

The green light began to flash. The assistant pilot tapped the first pair on their shoulders and Alex watched them shuffle over to the side and then throw themselves out. For a moment they were there, frozen in the doorway. Then they were gone, like a photograph crumpled and spun away by the wind. Two more men followed, then another two, until only the final pair had still to jump.

From *Stormbreaker* **by Anthony Horowitz**

1   Turn over the book and sketch the image you have in your mind. Label it. Don't worry about the quality of the drawing but notice what is where, and how far away it is.

2   Afterwards, check your drawing against the text – what was suggested by the words in the extract and what did you add of your own?

3   Which are the strongest, most memorable images in the extract and what makes them distinct?

4   How far away are you from the action and where do you seem to watch it from? Check to see if others have a similar viewing position. Can you account for the similarity?

5   Find the words in the text that fix you in your viewing position.

6   Rewrite the events from a point of view close to the assistant pilot, starting:

The assistant pilot scrambled out of the cockpit and entered the cabin where the paratroopers...

7   Rewrite the events from a point of view close to a paratrooper who jumps out in the third pair, starting:

Up at the front, the assistant pilot had entered the cabin and began...

Helping the reader's imagination

Writers can help the imagination by prompting the reader to think about:

- similar experiences in their own life
- their senses of sound, smell, feel, look and taste
- their personal memories
- their knowledge of history, geography and society
- stories they have seen, heard or read before.

Notice these techniques at work in this extract from a spy thriller:

Murder in the breaker's yard

Ian Rider hadn't died in any accident. What had killed him was plain to see – even to someone who had never seen such a thing before. A spray of bullets had caught the car full on the driver's side, shattering the front tyre, then smashing the windscreen and side windows and punching into the side panels. The metal felt cold against his flesh. He opened the door and looked inside. The front seats, pale grey leather, were strewn with fragments of broken glass and stained with patches of dark brown. He didn't need to ask what the stains were. He could see everything. The flash of the machine-gun, the bullets ripping into the car…

From *Stormbreaker* by Anthony Horowitz

Activity

1   Where in this extract do *your* memories come into play?

2   The writer holds back two pieces of information so that the reader is forced to draw conclusions. What are they?

3   Which senses are brought into play?

Activity

Describe, in five sentences, a car being crushed so that it is easy for your reader to imagine it.

> **1**
> Close your eyes and imagine it through as many of your five senses as possible.

> **2**
> Re-run the image slowly and see some more details.

> **3**
> Pick out three striking details to include in your writing.

> **4**
> Convert some of the sounds and movements into strong precise verbs.

> **5**
> Decide what each of the five sentences will be about and how each one will start.

>> Test it

Your test task is to imagine that a huge claw now grabs the car and the boy inside it is lifted into the air as the car swings over to the crusher. Describe the seconds in which this happens, and how he escapes. Help your readers to use their imaginations.

What you get marks for

Using at least three senses	2 marks
Using visual hints such as colour, shade, etc.	2 marks
Using striking details	2 marks
Emphasising or repeating key images	2 marks
Positioning the reader carefully to see what happens	2 marks
Total	**10 marks**

You can read the full scene in Chapter 2 of Anthony Horowitz's action novel *Stormbreaker*.

4. Establishing a voice

In this masterclass you will learn how to:

- find a comfortable writing voice
- put on a voice to suit the task
- establish a relationship with the reader.

Sometimes you have to adapt your own voice to suit the reader or the task. In **style**, you have to decide where your voice will be pitched between:

formal	informal
personal	impersonal
assertive	reticent
sophisticated	plain
conventional	unconventional

You can choose to be a **narrator** who:

- speaks in the first person (as 'I')
- speaks directly to the reader (using 'you')
- is a character in their own right
- stays invisible
- sticks close to one of the characters
- behaves like God and sees into the minds and motives of the characters.

A narrator who is a character in the story reveals their character in the way they tell the story, the comments they make and the attitudes they express. When you write 'in character' it is known as adopting a **persona**.

Finding your writing voice

Finding your own writing voice is an important discovery. Seek a style which fits well with your speaking voice. It should be clear, simple and versatile, good for school work and good for formal essays.

Have you found a comfortable personal style yet? If not, try this:

Step 1 – Strip back

- Strip back your style by writing in short sentences and choosing plain words.
- Be as brief, clear and specific as possible. Choose plain, accurate words.

Step 2 – Rehearse

- Run through the whole of what you are going to write in your head. Imagine yourself speaking to sympathetic adults. Hear how it would sound in your own best, clearest voice.
- Rehearse each sentence aloud in your head before you write. Always know how the sentence will end before you start writing. If you can't hold it all in your head, then at least decide on the structure of the sentence before you start.

Step 4 – Extend sentences

- Start joining up your short sentences, but don't settle for a long list of ANDs. Compress short sentences together into one richer sentence, or use subordinate clauses instead.

Step 3 – Strengthen sentences

- Pay attention to the verbs. Choose strong, clear ones.
- Vary your sentences by starting sometimes with *how*, *when*, *where* or *why* things happen.
- Increase the amount of description and reflection in your writing.

Activity

1 Find a piece of writing which felt clumsy or uncomfortable when you wrote it.

2 Try rewriting part of it in a more relaxed personal voice.

Writers say:

Every writer is a frustrated actor who recites his lines in the hidden auditorium of his skull.

Rod Sterling

The writer is a person who talks to himself, or better, who talks *in* himself.

Malcolm Cowley

A writer wastes nothing.

F. Scott Fitzgerald

It helps to read the sentence aloud.

Harry Kemelman

It's the writing that teaches you. It's the rotten stories that make it possible for you to write the good stories eventually.

Isaac Asimov

Blot out, correct, insert, refine,
Enlarge, diminish, interline;
Be mindful when invention fails,
To scratch your head, and bite your nails.

Jonathan Swift

**Jonathan Swift, author
of *Gulliver's Travels***

Putting on a voice

Experience may tell you the kind of voice to use in a piece of writing. But if you don't know, then you have to work it out.

Activity

1   Discuss how you would adapt your usual writing voice for the following writing tasks:

  • Explaining to a class of infants why they should not leave the classroom before they are collected at the end of the day.

  • Writing your personal targets for next term.

  • Applying for a Saturday job at a department store.

  • Evaluating another group's performance in drama.

  • Reporting the defeat of the school team in the area final.

2   Identify what it is in your writing voice that you can change to suit different tasks. Make a list. Check your answers at the end of this masterclass.

Activity

1   What impression do you get of the narrators in the next two extracts?

2   Pinpoint what it was in the content that gave rise to your impressions.

3   Pinpoint what it was in the voices that confirmed your impression.

T R E N D   W A T C H

Paradise regained

They grew on us last year, but this spring they're in full bloom. Yes, big surfer florals are in this year, and, yes, we're speaking to men here. Celine sent flowery prints down the runways and, on the high street, Diesel is leading the way with shirts (£60) and tees adorned with paradise island florals. Or check out the Mavi stand at Selfridges for £45 T-shirts, although we can't accept responsibility for your reputation if you go for Mavi's sarong *pour homme* (£35).

Natasha Polyviou

© Time Out Group 2004

'You'll never be able to follow *Christmas*,' said a friend after my last book and television series. 'It's such a special time for people who cook, and whatever you do now it won't have that same magic.'

Well, I've always been the kind of person who loves a challenge, so here I am. A hard act to follow it may be, but Christmas comes and then it goes, leaving us with a whole year in between. Of course, none of us, I suspect, would care to indulge ourselves in quite the same way more than once a year.

Summer, in my opinion, is an equally special time for cooks, a dazzling time when fresh ingredients present themselves.

From *Delia Smith's Summer Collection*

Activity

Do a quick survey of the contents of your class's lunchboxes, then write three short contrasting paragraphs reporting on your findings from the point of view of:

- an enthusiastic vegetarian
- a depressed dentist
- a hungry friend who's forgotten his or her own lunch.

>> Test it

Your test task is to write three paragraphs introducing your new book: **Table manners for young ladies and gentlemen**, in which you explain why it is your mission in life to bring etiquette back to the table.

You could start:

Since Nanny first drew up my high chair to the table, I have adored good table manners...

What you get marks for

Putting clues about the narrator's background into the content	2 marks
Using language that fits the aristocratic background	2 marks
Using a style that suggests formality and what is proper	2 marks
Avoiding language that is colloquial, over-personal, crude or rude	2 marks
Using an elegant style, no matter what is said	2 marks
Total	**10 marks**

ANSWERS

Things you can change

Your role, e.g. guide, friend, instructor.

The perspective, e.g. first person, third person.

The register, e.g. formal, impersonal, colloquial.

The tone, e.g. aggressive, patronising, sombre.

The style, e.g. elaborate, plain, literary.

The implied character behind the voice, e.g. personality, attitudes, opinions.

5. Managing vocabulary

In this masterclass you will learn:

- what to do when you don't know the right word
- strategies for remembering technical terms
- how to explain complex things.

What to do when you don't know the right word

The French have an expression *mot juste* which means just the right word in just the right place. Sometimes when you write you will be searching for a word and not know it or not remember it. Then you have to find a way to remember or replace the word.

Activity

Consider what strategies you would use in the following situations:

1   You have written:

> The giraffe's neck has been stretched to reach the highest leaves.

You don't like the phrase *has been stretched* because it sounds as though you had the animal on a rack and stretched it deliberately. How could you re-express it to get rid of this impression?

2   You are writing a geography essay but you have forgotten the exact word used by the teacher to describe the type of rainforest:

> The ????????????? rainforest is dense, dark and steamy.

You remember that the word was long and you think it began with E. How could you go about remembering, finding or substituting for this word?

3 You are writing about an archaeological find:

Archaeologists have unearthed a stone cylinder which has funny marks around it that prove that someone once tooled it thousands of years ago.

The phrase *funny marks* is vague and ambiguous. It doesn't tell you what the marks look like. Find a specific word or a short expression that describes the marks more accurately and indicates that they prove that it was once tooled.

4 You are writing about drilling tools in DT:

The ??????? holds the drill bit firmly in place so that it cuts a straight clean hole.

You can't remember the word for this part of the drill. Reorder the sentence to avoid having to use it. Find the correct term at the end of this masterclass.

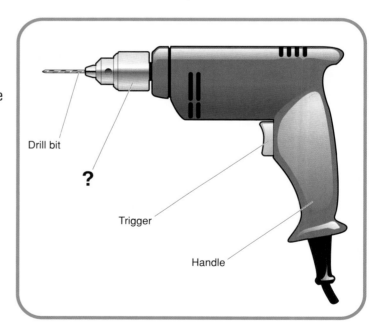

Drill bit

?

Trigger

Handle

Help ▶▶

What to do when you can't remember the word

- Say it in your own words.
- Trigger your memory by searching for synonyms (different words for the same thing).
- Run over the root words that might be used in it.
- Rephrase the sentence to avoid using it. Moving from active to passive usually works.
- Look it up in a thesaurus, using a word that comes close to the same meaning.
- Look it up in an encyclopaedia or textbook.
- Ask someone who does know.
- Start your sentence in a different way. This sometimes offers a new way of expressing the tricky section.

5 The music teacher has asked you to learn the meanings and spellings of the parts of a guitar.

Find ways of remembering the terms and how to spell them.

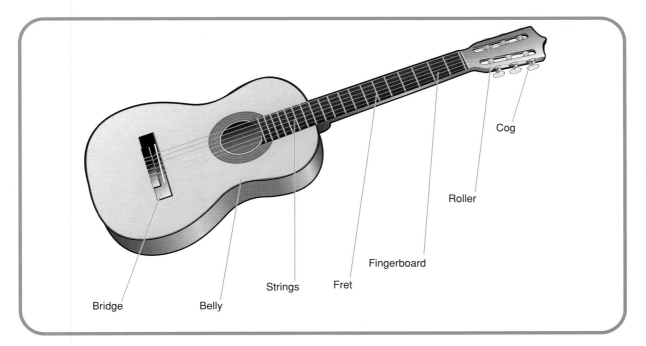

Help »

Remembering technical vocabulary

1 Take time to learn new terms when you meet them. Learn the spelling and meaning together.

2 Make a note of the term. Draw a tiny sketch against the word. Stick it on the wall next to your bed for one week. You will never forget it!

3 Use an image that ties the term and the thing together.
For example:

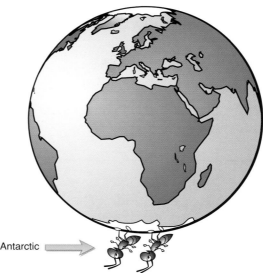

Antarctic →

4 Look for hints in the word that will help you to remember the meaning and spelling. For example:

A **vein** carries blood into the heart, and an **artery** carries blood away from the heart.

Ve**IN**   Artery
IN   Away

5 Test yourself every time you see it. Mentally label it.

Explaining complex things

This junction in Swindon is known by local people as the Magic Roundabout. It started as a joke but the council have now put up a sign using the term as its official name.

There is not an accepted term for this kind of roundabout. Can you invent a term that would give people the right idea, even without a diagram?

In two or three sentences, explain how the roundabout works. (You need to know that drivers approaching a roundabout must give way to cars already on it. You always turn left into a roundabout.)

Having the right technical word is helpful because:

- there is no room for misunderstanding
- it saves complicated explanations
- it is short.

When you use technical terms:

- don't bother introducing them as a textbook would, but just use them
- keep the rest of your language simple
- chunk up the explanation
- vary the way you start explaining each step.

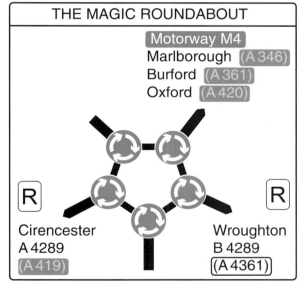

Help ▶▶

Explaining complex things

Use the following sequence to explain complex things:

1 Explain its purpose
2 Describe it
3 Explain the principle on which it works
4 Illustrate with an example
5 Give other essential information (if any)
6 Summarise 'in a nutshell' how it works.

>> Test it

Use the diagram to explain how a toilet flushes.

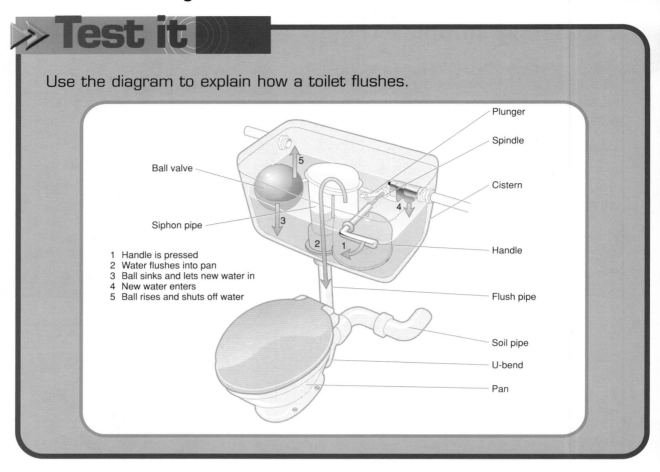

Plunger

Spindle

Ball valve

Cistern

4

Siphon pipe

Handle

1 Handle is pressed
2 Water flushes into pan
3 Ball sinks and lets new water in
4 New water enters
5 Ball rises and shuts off water

Flush pipe

Soil pipe

U-bend

Pan

What you get marks for

An explanation that is easy to follow	2 marks
Using clear and simple language	2 marks
Using the technical terms accurately	2 marks
Using technical terms with ease	2 marks
Chunking up the explanation and varying the starts	2 marks
Total	**10 marks**

ANSWERS

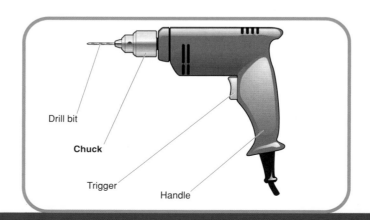

Drill bit

Chuck

Trigger

Handle

6. Getting more from your words

In this masterclass you will learn how to:

- get more from your nouns
- get more from your verbs
- get more from the position of key words in a sentence.

Getting more from your nouns

To get more from your nouns, you can:

- **Make them more specific**. For example:

  Writer ⟶ scriptwriter
  Musician ⟶ violinist
  House ⟶ bungalow

- **Add adjectives**. For example:

  She had an idea. ⟶ She had an <u>original</u> idea.
  He was a waiter. ⟶ He was an <u>experienced</u> waiter.
  He was a writer. ⟶ He was a writer <u>of little talent</u>.

- **Use simile or metaphor**. For example:

  <u>Like ants</u>, shoppers swarmed into the shops.
  He was a publishing <u>giant</u>.
  She feared that his <u>clownish</u> behaviour would get him into trouble.

- **Define them with a telling detail**. For example:

  He fell with a crash onto the floor. ⟶
  He fell with a crash onto <u>the metal plates of the walkway</u>.
  She wore a warm coat. ⟶ She wore a warm <u>cashmere jacket</u>.
  He froze at the sight of the gun in Franz's fist. ⟶ He froze at the <u>sudden glint of gunmetal in Franz's fist</u>.

Getting more from your verbs

To get more from your verbs, you can:

● **Make them more specific**. For example:

Went ⟶ proceeded, journeyed, hiked
Said ⟶ whispered, proclaimed, queried
Got ⟶ acquired, received, retrieved

● **Make them metaphorical**. For example:

She <u>said</u>, 'Never!' ⟶ 'Never!' she <u>snorted</u>.
He <u>moved sideways</u> across the rocks. ⟶ He <u>crabbed</u> across the rocks.
He <u>became</u> more and more angry. ⟶ He <u>steamed</u> with anger.

● **Make them stronger**. For example:

The dog was <u>eating</u> its bone. ⟶ The dog was <u>gnawing</u> on a bone.
She <u>asked</u> him to stop. ⟶ She <u>implored</u> him to stop.
Dinosaurs <u>became larger</u>. ⟶ Dinosaurs <u>developed into huge creatures</u>.

● **Make them onomatopoeiac**. For example:

The papers <u>crackled</u> as the flames consumed them.
She <u>soothed</u> and <u>hushed</u> the baby into sleep.
The plates <u>clattered</u> as they were laid rapidly on the tables.

● **Add adverbs**. For example:

They sang <u>tunelessly</u>.
They fought <u>without hope</u>.
They traded information <u>discreetly and profitably</u>.

● **Use two for effect**. For example:

They <u>spluttered and coughed</u> in the smoke.
They <u>heaved and dragged</u> the sacks across the barn.
The last firework <u>sizzled and wailed</u> in the night sky.

Activity

1   Study the nouns and verbs in the following paragraph about a prisoner of war who has just escaped from a prison camp. Reword it as indicated to strengthen the sense of age, risk and loneliness.

A prisoner of war on the run

Ted got (improve this verb) behind the (add an adjective) bush growing against the rear wall of the mill. A window in the wall was broken. He looked (improve this verb) through it. The mill was clearly no longer used. An old (improve this adjective) cart stood in the centre of the building. Beneath the window were piled (improve this verb) old seed boxes and a pile of old (improve this adjective) flour sacks. Some (add an adjective) buckets, one of them containing an old (improve this adjective) grain scoop, lay on their sides by the double door and various lengths of rope were loosely piled (improve this verb) here and there. On the floor to one side of the window was a pile of bat droppings showing (improve this verb) that no-one (improve this noun) regularly came to (improve this verb) the place.

- Once you have finished, find the original passage at the end of this masterclass.
- Remember that you were asked to increase the sense of age, risk and loneliness. How did you do compared with the original writer?

2   Improve this paragraph in the same way:

Taking a direct hit at sea

The floor under Ted's feet shook and moved. Hot air burned his face and blew him against Sharkey who tripped and only stayed on his feet by holding onto the gun. Where the torpedo tube has been, smoke was coming from a hole in the deck.

You can find the original at the end of this masterclass.

Getting more from the position of key words in a sentence

The position of words in a sentence can give them extra meaning or force. The best place is always the one that helps the meaning of the sentence. For example, you can:

- keep the reader in suspense by putting a key word at the end
- surprise the reader by putting an unexpected word at the end
- grab the reader's attention by starting with a high-impact word
- build up to the key word, then extend the sentence with fascinating details about it
- mimic the sequence of actions in the structure of the sentence.

Activity

Find six examples of key words or expressions in this extract that have been carefully positioned to give them extra value.

A case of frostbite

The other prisoners gathered round, watching. One put his hand on the Russian's shoulder and said, 'You'll be all right matey,' yet the Russian showed no sign of recognition. He just kept staring at the stove close to which Pete Dodd held two blankets, warming them.

Finally, Ted reached the end of the Russian's foot and slid the sock free. The toes were as black as one of the pieces of charred wood in the fire, the nails peeling upwards from the flesh.

'Frozen solid,' a voice said quietly.

Ted took hold of the Russian's leg to lower it to the floor. As he did so, he brushed the big toe against the side of his thigh. The toe broke off, fell to the floor and rolled away. Ted stared at it until it came to rest against one of the legs of the stove: then he passed out.

By midday, the young Russian soldier was dead.

From *POW* by Martin Booth

1 Explain how each of your six key words from the extract on the opposite page has earned extra value from its position in the sentence.

2 Find two examples of repeated key words or expressions and what they add.

Activity

Reorganise the words in the sentences of this paragraph to emphasise the sudden change in the weather because spring is on the way.

The sudden arrival of spring

The weather suddenly warmed up in early April. The last vestiges of snow disappeared overnight and the thin glazing of ice melted around the edge of the lake. The mauve and orange spears of crocus flowers were pushing through the soil within days in the lawn of the German officers' beer garden, close by their accommodation building. The buds began to burst outside the perimeter fence and the trees became hazed with green.

You can find the writer's original at the end of this masterclass.

Write three exciting paragraphs describing one man's escape from a prison camp. Make good use of nouns and verbs and the organisation of sentences.

What you get marks for

A good choice of strong verbs	2 marks
Enhancing the verbs, e.g. with adverbs, onomatopoeia	2 marks
A good choice of effective nouns	1 mark
Enhancing the nouns, e.g. with details, adjectives	2 marks
Positioning key words to good effect	3 marks
Total	**10 marks**

ANSWERS

Ted slipped behind the holly bush growing against the rear wall of the mill. A window in the wall was broken. He peered through it. The mill was clearly no longer used. A derelict cart stood in the centre of the building. Beneath the window were stacked old seed boxed and a pile of rotting flour sacks. Some wooden buckets, one of them containing a rusting grain scoop, lay on their sides by the double door and various lengths of rope were loosely coiled here and there. On the floor to one side of the window was a pile of bat droppings testifying that no humans regularly visited the place.

Suddenly, the deck under Ted's feet shivered and rippled as if it were made of cardboard. A blast of searing air scorched his cheeks and threw him against Sharkey who stumbled and only stayed on his feet by grasping the hold of the breech mechanism lever of the gun. Where the torpedo tube has been, thick, oily smoke was belching from a jagged hole in the deck plates.

Early in April, the weather suddenly warmed. Overnight, the last vestiges of snow disappeared and the thin glazing of ice around the edge of the lake melted. Within days, the mauve and orange spears of crocus flowers were pushing through the soil in the lawn of the German officers' beer garden, close by their accommodation building. Outside the perimeter fence, the trees became hazed with green as their buds began to burst.

All from *POW* by Martin Booth

7. Extending your sentences

In this masterclass, you will learn how to extend your sentences by:

● linking several actions, ideas or objects
● adding in further detail
● starting with adverbial information.

Linking ideas

Writers often choose to roll actions or objects together into one sentence so that the reader 'sees' them together. A single compressed sentence can be richer and shorter than three separate sentences. Notice how each of the following sentences has rolled together a number of separate things:

A mountain rescue

Even in the very cold weather I wore just a pair of trousers, boots and a T-shirt with a waterproof over the top.

The standby squadron got up onto the hill and found the body, but they couldn't get down because the weather was so bad.

When the weather cleared they laid him on his back, piled their bergens on top, and sledged him down the hill.

From *Immediate Action* by Andy McNab

Notice the 'snapshot' that is created by rolling together two or three things into each sentence. It works like any list: items are linked by commas or a conjunction such as 'and' or 'but'.

Activity

Try linking these four sentences by rolling them into one 'snapshot':

They found him in his sleeping bag.   **He had biscuits in one hand.**
He was half in and half out of it.   **He had a hexy burner in the other.**

You can find the writer's original sentence at the end of this masterclass.

Revealing details

Adding on a revealing detail is a useful strategy for making a scene real, particular and memorable. For example:

> I recall a sensation of utter sickness, a feeling as if my brain were upside down within my skull.

> The line of the cliff was marked by strange reddish shapes, tongues of vermilion flame that writhed and danced.

> Something was at work upon my face, some thin feelers worried my ears.

From *The First Men in the Moon* by H.G. Wells

Notice how:

- Each one starts with a mini-sentence to which details are added.
- The first part is general and the second part is more specific and sharp.
- There is a comma between the main sentence and the added detail.

Activity

Add a revealing detail to these sentence starters to impress upon the reader the woman's great age:

She was older than I'd imagined,...
Her face was etched with deep lines,...
I watched her approach,...

Zooming in

If you add on more than one detail, it acts like a zoom lens does on a camera. Imagine the film version of these sentences:

> The child was asleep, the eyelids not quite shut, showing a slight film of black pupil between.
>
> From *The Rainbow* by D.H. Lawrence

> All the streets were lined with stalls loaded with food in heaps, chiefly dried fish, the entrails of animals, and gingerbread.
>
> From *The Old Wives' Tale* by Arnold Bennett

> I caught a second glimpse of things outside, puffs of vapour, half-liquid slush, excavated, sliding, falling, sliding.
>
> From *The First Men in the Moon* by H.G. Wells

Activity

1 What was the lens in your mind doing?

2 Add three extra details to each of these sentence starters:

I slumped down onto the bunk of my new cell,...

(add details that tell the reader how you feel)

The battlefield lay all around us,...

(add chilling details that suggest what has just happened there)

The girls spent lunchtime lazing by the tennis courts,...

(add details about what they were doing)

> **Hot Tip**
>
> If you get stuck, try starting with a word ending in *-ing* or *-ed*, e.g. feeling, covered or chatting.

The piling on of extra details is a technique writers use to suggest either depth (going in closer) or plenty (taking in a variety of things). It is especially useful when you are describing a scene.

Adding in extra sentences

Sentences can also be extended by adding in another sentence or two. There's no point in doing this unless there is value in pulling two ideas together into one sentence.

The word *and* can be used to hitch two sentences together, but it doesn't add anything at all to the meaning. More useful are conjunctions that tell you what the relationship is between the first sentence and the second. For example:

although – warns you that a reservation is about to be expressed

until – warns you that a time limit is about to be issued

unless – warns you that a condition is about to be set

without – warns you that something is about to be excluded

because – warns you that a reason is about to be given

Notice how the writer extends sentences here to mention something else that happens at the same time. He uses conjunctions to pull two sentences together so that you see them happening at the same time.

Shooting an elephant

When I pulled the trigger I did not hear the bang or feel the kick – one never does when a shot goes home – <u>but</u> I heard the devilish roar of glee that went up from the crowd. In that instant, in too short a time, one would have thought, even for the bullet to get there, a mysterious, terrible change had come over the elephant. He neither stirred nor fell, <u>but</u> every line of his body had altered. He looked suddenly stricken, shrunken, immensely old, <u>as though</u> the frightful impact of the bullet had paralysed him without knocking him down. At last, after what seemed a long time – it might have been five seconds, I dare say – he sagged flabbily to his knees. His mouth slobbered.

From *Shooting an Elephant* by George Orwell

Placing in context

Here is a way of extending a sentence at the beginning. A good way to get your reader in the right frame of mind is to start by getting them to think about **when**, **where**, **how** or **why** something happens. This can be done very simply:

> **At the first sound of footsteps on the stairs**, he slipped the book under the pillow and ran across to the light switch.
>
> **With the door open**, he relaxed and paused on the step to listen.
>
> **As he climbed**, his feet and hands dislodged a tickle of plaster and stone dust, and birds brushed his knuckles as they flashed out of their nest holes.
>
> **Very slowly and very carefully**, he tested each hold thoroughly before trusting it with his weight.
>
> **From *A Kestrel for a Knave* by Barry Hines**

Notice how each sentence opens with a phrase that tells you more about the verb, and this is why openers like these are called **adverbials**.

Activity

1 Go back to the extract *Shooting an elephant* opposite and find three sentences starting with an adverbial.

2 Go back to the last activity, and change the adverbials to do a different job. For example, if it says *where*, change it to an adverbial that says *how*, *why* or *when*.

Test it

Your test task is to extend the sentences below to create a vivid and detailed account of the end of the elephant described on page 40.

> I fired again. He did not collapse. He stood upright. I fired a third time. That was the shot that did for him. You could see the agony of it. He seemed to rise. He trumpeted. Then down he came.

What you get marks for

Using two adverbial starts	2 marks
Adding on details that zoom in	3 marks
Choosing details that are specific and revealing	2 marks
Linking ideas or things together in at least one snapshot sentence	2 marks
Leaving one or two sentences plain and direct for effect	1 mark
Total	**10 marks**

You can read the original below from *Shooting an Elephant* by George Orwell.

ANSWERS

Sleeping bag

They found him in his sleeping bag, half in, half out, with biscuits in one hand and a hexy burner in the other.

From *Immediate Action* by Andy McNab

Adverbials: The first, second and fifth sentences start with adverbials.

Shooting an elephant

I fired again into the same spot. At the second shot he did not collapse but climbed with desperate slowness to his feet and stood weakly upright, with legs sagging and head drooping. I fired a third time. That was the shot that did for him. You could see the agony of it jolt his whole body and knock the last remnant of strength from his legs. But in falling he seemed for a moment to rise, for as his hind legs collapsed beneath him he seemed to tower upwards like a huge rock toppling, his trunk reaching skywards like a tree.

From *Shooting an Elephant* by George Orwell

8. Developing your ideas

In this masterclass you will learn how to:

- map the structure and proportions of a piece of writing
- plan paragraphs
- unfold ideas in prose.

Mapping your writing

When you write, it is often easy to list the contents but not to see the proportions. For example, a travel writer may write about a journey across five countries, but not use the same amount of space on each one.

The writing plan for a journey

1	2	3	4	5	6	7
Intro	Brazil	Venezuela	Ecuador	Mexico	Peru	Conc

The same applies to telling a story. You don't have to give the same amount of space to each event. Instead, you can focus on the significant and interesting things.

The writing plan for a story

1	2	3	4	5	6	7
Opening – They meet after 5 years apart.	Flashback – When they met 6 years ago.	The assignment – They work together, old feelings reviving?	Flashback – When they were deeply in love.	A problem develops – They become irritable with each other.	Flashback – The months of irritation and tension before they split up.	End of day – Both know best to leave things as they are.

Activity

Re-draw the proportions you would give to these sequences

1   An account of a field trip.

1	2	3	4	5	6	7
Factual info about the valley trip.	The journey there.	The steep climb up to the spring which is the source of the river.	The upper valley – rills, rocks and waterfalls.	The middle valley – the river, the riverbanks, wildlife living by the river.	The lower river – the flood plain, pasture, agriculture, marshland and tidal features.	The mouth of the river – the town, industrial pollution.

2   A homework assignment about the experience of being blind. You were asked to spend one hour in a blindfold at the weekend.

1	2	3	4	5	6	7
First minute – immediately realise how difficult it is going to be – all the things you can't do easily.	Finding my way around – tripping, knowing where things are.	Simple things are difficult – how I coped at lunch, toilet, putting on shoes.	Dangers, obstacles, knives, fires, the dog!	How other people reacted and coped – hard to be independent.	What I couldn't do – reading, TV, video, computer, see what people were talking about, etc.	What was better – sounds, radio, conversation, touch.

Planning your paragraphs

Once you have decided the relative proportion of each section, you have to move on to imagining how it will 'play out'. For example:

Story section 5
A problem develops – They become irritable with each other.

Paragraph 1: Digging together when they make a find.
Dialogue: Slight tension over whose 'find' it is.
Paragraph 2: She is put out when others offer congratulations to him.
Paragraph 3: Further tension when he is invited to meet the sponsor but she is not.

That section will eventually become a side of writing and will consist of at least three big paragraphs plus a few lines of dialogue. A good writer will see how important it is that the dialogue reveals an awkward tension emerging, and that the following paragraphs show rather than tell the developing rift between the man and woman. In the next story section, the writer will go on to show how a similar tension existed in the past and led to their break up.

Another example:

Field trip section 4
The upper valley – rills, rocks and waterfalls.

Paragraph 1: Description of the landscape – steep, rocky valley cut by river.

Paragraph 2: The river – small fast-flowing streams gathering and forming tributaries to main river, cutting riverbed, steep falls over clefts in the rock.

Paragraph 3: Flora and fauna – rock-climbing animals (sheep and goats) – but little pasture to support them. Too cold for many plants, and not much soil – just alpines, heathers, etc.

The big decision lies in deciding the topics for each paragraph. But there are other ways of doing it. For example:

Field trip section 4 (alternative version)
The upper valley – rills, rocks and waterfalls.

Paragraph 1: The peaks – desolate, support very few plants, rain gathers and runs downhill.

Paragraph 2: The cliffs – small fast-flowing streams gather, cut into the rock and form waterfalls over clefts in the rock; goats and a few alpine plants survive.

Paragraph 3: High land – more grass, heather and flowers – supports sheep – streams gather into tributaries which rush down to the main river cutting deep into the rock.

Activity

Write a three-paragraph plan for:

1   Section 6 of the story.
2   Section 6 of the blindfold activity.

Developing ideas

Ideas take shape in different ways. Once you are writing you will find that some ideas come easily and seem obvious. Yet each new paragraph offers the opportunity to change tack. Before you begin writing the paragraph, it is helpful if you know roughly how it will go.

Thinking time

- Take a moment of thinking time before you get stuck into a paragraph.

- In your mind, run over the different ways you could take it.

- Choose a strategy or approach, e.g. description giving way to reflection; action followed by description.

- Voice the opening words to check that they will lead you off in the right direction. Always consider how to capture the attention of the reader.

- Have a mental map of how the paragraph will unfold, even if you do not have the words yet.

- Many writers find it helpful to decide in advance how the paragraph will end, and often have the exact words. They find it easier to write when they know the ending.

Activity

1 In the story plan on page 43, how would you go about showing what happened in the flashback in section 4? You know that you don't want to spend long on it so it needs to be a moment that says it all. What will it be?

2 In the account of being blindfolded on page 44, how would you go about explaining how difficult it was to find your way about in section 2? There's a lot you could say. Do you just list some things that were difficult? Or do you illustrate the point by recounting a couple of difficulties you encountered in the first five minutes, perhaps in an amusing way? Do a paragraph plan like those on pages 44–5.

3 You are both the narrator and the hero in a long epic journey with many trials and battles. After a particularly fierce battle in which two comrades have been slaughtered, you and your friends rest on the banks of a wide river which you must later cross. Plan and then write the paragraph about your thoughts and feelings during this brief period of rest.

4 You are in the middle of hand-to-hand combat when you notice with great anxiety that an important object – a ring, a letter or a dagger – has been dropped on the ground and is becoming lost in the undergrowth. Plan and write a paragraph in which these two things happen simultaneously – the fight and the lost object.

5 You are writing about the impact of email on people's lives and there are many things to cover: the way email has undermined post and telephone services; the way it is fast; the informal style that is accepted; the inconvenience of having to log on; the fact many people do not have email addresses; and the way it depends on good keyboard skills. But how do you organise the paragraph given that the points could be made in almost any order? Plan and then write it.

Your test task is to:

1   Write a paragraph plan for the last section of the story on page 43.

2   Write the last two sections of the story using the paragraph plans you made for them.

What you get marks for

A two- or three-paragraph plan with clear solid ideas that will be useful when it comes to writing up   3 marks

A story that is shown or 'dramatised' rather than narrated   3 marks

Writing in paragraphs that reflect shifts in topic, time or perspective   2 marks

The overall effect – a story that seems interesting and well-written   2 marks

Total   **10 marks**

C. HITTING THE RIGHT NOTE

9. The assertive voice

In this masterclass you will learn how to:

- sound confident
- write assertively
- deal confidently with objections.

The ring of confidence

It is important to sound confident when:

- the matter is urgent and important
- you wish to inspire trust and confidence
- you are in charge and people are looking to you for a lead
- if you don't insist, it won't happen
- you are addressing someone who tends to ignore you.

Confidence is more than attitude; it shows in the language you use. You can have an air of confidence if you know the right language.

Activity

Spend three or four minutes in a small group discussing when you felt it necessary to sound confident and how you did it. Discuss the kind of language you used to speak or write on those occasions.

Help ≫

Simple techniques for sounding confident

1 Use words that signal confidence:

certainly

naturally

obviously

clearly

of course

2 Use plain direct sentences.

3 Use strong plain verbs.

4 Be friendly but formal.

Assertive writing

On the opposite page is a public health leaflet warning about a cancer that is often ignored. It is written in an assertive voice to emphasise the importance and urgency of the warning. It is, after all, a matter of life or death.

Activity

Study the language used in the leaflet. Point to the features that make the voice so assertive.

Consider:

At word level:

- the choice of words and expressions
- the use of repetition and other techniques
- the level of formality, technicality or complexity.

At sentence level:

- the length and expression of sentences
- the choice and position of verbs
- the way the writer's voice addresses the reader.

At text level:

- the tone taken
- the structure and organisation of the whole
- how the key messages are emphasised.

You will notice that the language is similar to that used in persuasive writing such as advertising or 'point of view' work. That is because it is a form of promotion. However, assertive writing does not need to 'sell' or exaggerate its claims. Indeed, in public health this might lead people to ignore small symptoms. So assertive writing is accurate in content but forceful in tone.

Activity

Use an assertive style in a one-sided leaflet to warn older primary school children about personal safety when they are out on their own.

sun know how

FACT CARD

- Skin cancer is the second most common cancer in the UK
- The number of new cases increases every year and has doubled in the past 20 years
- The cause of skin cancer is nearly always over exposure to ultraviolet radiation – from the sun or a sunbed
- Ultraviolet radiation is reflected off light coloured surfaces, especially water, sand and snow – this increases it's strength
- You can still get sunburnt through light cloud or under shallow water – protect yourself when swimming
- There is nothing healthy about a suntan. Your skin darkens because it has been damaged
- Most cases of skin cancer could be easily prevented

PROTECT YOURSELF AND FOLLOW THE SUN SAFETY CODE

COVER UP – with loose, cool clothing to keep the sun off your skin. Wear a hat, preferably with a wide brim and sunglasses (BS2724:1987)

PROTECT CHILDREN – they are particularly vulnerable. Sunburn during childhood can lead to skin cancer later in life. Keep babies out of the sun completely.

SEEK SHADE – especially during the hottest part of the day, from 11am to 3pm.

USE A SUNSCREEN – SPF 15 or higher on any exposed skin. Use it an hour before going outside and reapply it frequently and generously.

TAKE CARE NOT TO BURN – sunburn increases your risk of skin cancer

Sun Know How Fact Card
© Crown Copyright

BE AWARE OF YOUR SKIN. If you have a mole that is changing size, shape, colour, itching or bleeding – see your doctor. If skin cancers are treated early, they should cause you no further problems.

TAKE SPECIAL CARE:

- Of children and babies, they spend longer outdoors and burn easily
- If you have very pale skin, fair or red hair
- If you have a lot of moles or freckles
- If you have had skin cancer before, or you have a family history of it
- If you work or spend a lot of time outdoors

FACT: Brown or black skinned people rarely get skin cancer, however they should still take care in the hot sun.

FACT: The sun also causes thickening of the skin leading to premature ageing and wrinkles.

FACT: Too much sun can also cause heat exhaustion, skin irritation and sun stroke – especially in the very young.

Enjoy the sun but take it easy – skin cancer kills approximately 2000 people every year in the UK.

sun know how

Pre-empting objections

Good assertive writing avoids problems by pre-empting objections. This means tackling problems before someone else raises them.

Activity

Despite warnings, many people ignore advice about sun protection. They believe it doesn't count in their case. The writer of the leaflet on the previous page knows some of the myths about skin cancer and tries to tackle them before people object. Can you spot them?

Check your answers at the end of this masterclass.

Responding to objections

Sometimes you have to respond to complaints, counter-arguments and objections.

Firstly, keep your cool.

Secondly, acknowledge anything that is true in what they say. This shows you are listening, and it is courteous. It makes you look reasonable.

Hot Tip ▶▶

Keeping your cool
- Keep an even tone.
- Stick to your own pace – don't rush.
- Avoid sharp words.
- Acknowledge strong feelings.
- Don't wilt or get apologetic.

Thirdly, reply to the objection in one of these ways:

- Show that the facts are right but the conclusion is wrong.
- Show that the facts are wrong so the conclusion can't be trusted.
- Find evidence against it.
- Find a flaw in the logic.
- Show how the solution would lead to other problems the writer didn't mention.
- Show that it is outweighed by the arguments against it.

Activity

Study the Help box on the right and follow the advice above to reply to the objections below:

Objection 1

All my friends sunbathe and none of them ever get ill as a result. The risk must be so tiny!

Objection 2

We're always being told that things are bad for us. There's a new scare every week. If we avoided everything, we'd never go out, we'd never try anything new and we'd never eat. It's not practical to worry about every little thing.

Objection 3

I don't earn enough money to go on sunshine holidays, so I don't have to worry about it.

Sounding reasonable

1 Acknowledge the views expressed even if you don't agree with them.
2 Keep your language polite and pleasant.
3 Stay calm and logical.
4 Claim the majority for your opinion:
   Most people agree that...
   No one wishes to...
5 Signal that you keep an open mind:
   Until we know more, I think we should...
   A good compromise would be to...

≫ Test it

Your test task is to use the following notes to write a one-sided leaflet of safety advice for young backpackers. The notes outline the problems encountered by backpackers. Your task is to give them good advice that will keep them out of harm.

Why young people go backpacking – for fun, for adventure, to gain experience after school but before starting work or university.

The scale of the problem – a third of all backpackers run into trouble, and young backpackers are twice as likely to have problems.

The commonest problems – having an accident; falling ill; being mugged for money or possessions, including mobile phones; getting beaten up when you fight back; getting cornered in backstreets and after dark; getting lost; being followed home and then robbed; breaking the law without realising it, thus getting into trouble with the police; missing a flight; getting caught up in riots; losing touch with friends and family.

but

'Most people do travel safely and come back with fantastic memories of their trip.'

Claire Southern of *Rough Guide*

What you get marks for

Using a confident, assertive voice	2 marks
Using bold verbs	1 mark
Using strong, direct sentences	2 marks
Giving a set of clear, reasonable instructions	2 marks
Pre-empting a couple of objections	2 marks
Alerting rather than terrifying your readers	1 mark
Total	**10 marks**

ANSWERS

Pre-empting objections:

- It doesn't matter if it's cloudy.
- It doesn't matter if you're under water.
- Surely suntans are healthy.
- Only old people get cancer.
- You only need one coat of suntan lotion.
- Only white people are at risk.

10. The discursive voice

In this masterclass you will learn how to:

- use language to explore ideas and issues
- use hypothesis and speculation as tools for writing
- represent a range of views when you write.

Activity

In a group, describe an occasion when you got into a deep argument or a deep discussion. Describe how the conversation developed.

- List some of the annoying phrases and tactics people use.
- List some of the constructive phrases and tactics people use.
- List some of the features of constructive discussion.

A **hypothesis** is an idea which you think may be true but you need to test it to be sure. A good way of testing an idea is to imagine how it would work in practice. **Speculation** is when you imagine the different ways things could turn out.

Activity

Spend five minutes testing these hypotheses by imagining how they would work in practice. Consider positives, negatives, possible consequences and things you would wish to research further.

1 Parents would improve if their children had the right to divorce them.
2 Age limits are worthless.

List the strategies you used to think through the implications.
For example:

- Running it over time: *at first...in the short term...in the medium term...in the long run...*
- Following a sequence of cause and effect: *if you do that, then this happens...and as a result...*
- Imagining the reactions of different people: *parents...children...brothers and sisters...*

List the form of words you used to test an idea. For example:
Supposing... What if...? But what about...?

Activity

1   Spend three minutes living in your mind, in real time, what would happen next if a small earthquake occurred right now.

2   Write a few paragraphs under the title *Shockwave* which describes the first 30 seconds of the event.

Imagination

The word *imagination* comes from the word *image*. People with good imaginations tend to visualise situations and act them out in their heads. They improvise in the way you would in a drama lesson, a computer action game or a daydream. Many writers plan their stories by playing them out in their head first. Have you tried this? Good times for the imagination are when you wake up or when you settle down in bed at night. Try living out an imaginary situation at one of these times.

Keeping your balance

When you present your own point of view in writing, you only have your own opinions to consider. If you are confident, you can tackle counter-arguments as you go. But on other occasions we are expected to report on other people's views on complex topics. This involves managing several points of view and presenting them in a balanced way.

Activity

Should dangerous sports be controlled and if so, how? Read the views and the case study on pages 57–8, and consider how you would plan an article which presents a balanced discussion of the issues. Write a paragraph plan for an article seven to nine paragraphs long. You can include quotations.

Dangerous sports

Prize fighter: I don't see why it's anyone's business but mine. If I want to take risks, that's my decision. I'm an adult. I can be called up to fight for my country, so why the hell should my country want to draw the line on my fighting for myself?

Sport business owner: This isn't just a few crackpots. Companies come to us for help with team-building. Even schools bring pupils here to challenge them and take them to the edge. These are not minority sports any more. We are fully booked.

Snowboarder: Okay, it's dangerous. I broke my shoulder and a rib a couple of years ago, but you have to expect to take some tumbles. I still go back. Why do I do it? For the rush, the adrenalin, the thrill, the experience.

Hospital porter in the Swiss alps: They're young and rich and bored. They have big egos and big wallets. They come up here with more money to spend than I make in a year, and go home with their broken legs and ribs and arms and boast about it. They have more money than sense. They're pathetic.

Son of free climber lost on peaks: I think that travel companies sell extreme sports as a holiday with a difference. People think it's scary but assume it is safe. If they realised how high the risks are, they would never go. No one told my father about the real risks. No one really trained him or informed him about the realities of what he was about to do.

Trainer: When people come up here, we check their health and fitness, and we train them in the skills they need. We do everything we can to keep it safe. There are trained helpers at every step. We don't want corpses on our hands; that just wouldn't be in our interests.

Case study: Death at a public fight

At Toughman events, participants pay an entry fee and sign up on the spot, getting into the ring after having their blood pressure and heart rate checked by a doctor.

Young signed up on a lark and, like many participants, had never fought before and had no training. Young, a 30-year-old mother of two, died on Tuesday, three days after she was beaten into a coma by a 20-year-old cake baker. She was the fourth Toughman fatality nationally in the last year.

Toughman promoter Art Dore did not return a call on Friday for comment, but he has said in a statement that his events are safer than other combat sports.

The bouts are sanctioned by a foundation Dore owns. He has been criticised nationwide for using inexperienced referees and improperly trained medical personnel to monitor the fights. The lawyer for Young's family says the doctor at her fight was taking photos and was not paying attention as she was being pummeled.

Extreme fighting events are supposed to be illegal in Florida, but Dore says his bouts are legal because of a loophole that leaves amateur boxing unregulated. Even if he were found to have broken the law, it's currently just a misdemeanor punishable by a small fine and short jail sentence.

From an article by Vickie Chachere of *Associated Press* on *polkonline.com*

Planning discursive writing

Things to avoid	Things to do
Just listing different opinions	Build your plan around the main talking points
Agree/disagree debates	Discuss the grey areas
Pushing your own opinion	Present the range of issues
Over-simplifying	Explain the complexities
Jumping to conclusions	Keep an open mind

1   Your main aim is to identify a handful of key issues around which to structure your essay. Go through the material and see if there are obvious issues.

For example, one is: *personal freedom to take risks*.

2   For each key issue, note down what you can say. For example, present the different views and try to explain them, give any examples or quotations, and above all, get to the nub of the argument. There is no need to be stuck for ideas if you go beyond the material provided and think for yourself. Your own ideas will glue together the various ideas and information. Try to get to the underlying principle. For example:

Personal freedom to take risks

- Enthusiasts claim it's their right (quote from enthusiast)
- They point to other risks that society accepts, e.g. smoking, crossing roads
- Seems hypocritical to ban sports but expect people to fight for country – a bigger risk to life
- Deaths are few anyway
- Currently, it is up to individuals to insure themselves
- Enthusiasts and companies agree that good safety training and preparation are essential (quote from trainer)
- Should society let people take foolish risks? Where does one draw the line? What counts as 'dangerous'?

Test it

Your test task is to write three paragraphs in which you explore the consequences of banning extreme sports.

What you get marks for

Identifying at least four possible consequences (0.5 mark each)	2 marks
Recognising the positive as well as the negative consequences	1 mark
Not forcing your own views on the reader	1 mark
The issues are discussed not just listed	2 marks
The points are well grouped and the links are clear	2 marks
The points of principle come out clearly	2 marks
Total	**10 marks**

11. Using humour

In this masterclass you will learn how to:

- exploit words for their humour
- use stylistic humour
- use gentle literary humour.

Humour in writing

A great deal of humour is **non-verbal**. Think of slapstick or comic sketches in which people get stuck in tricky situations. Think of the antics of Charlie Chaplin and circus clowns who work without words.

Even more humour is **oral**. The jokes that pass between friends and the use of repartee are examples. Impressionists who mimic famous people are also oral comedians.

Most of the humour you see on television or film is laughing at people in awkward situations (called **situation comedy**) or mocking their attitudes or manners (called the **comedy of manners**). Simple verbal humour depends on **wordplay**.

Activity

Can you match the type of wordplay with its definition and its example?

Type of wordplay	Explanation	Examples
1 Malapropism	**A** Playing on words with more than one meaning	**i** Gobstopper; knuckleduster; Justin Thyme.
2 Spoonerism	**B** Absurd misuse of a word because it sounds like another	**ii** When we argued he called me all the epitaphs he could.
3 Pun	**C** Witty use of words in an unexpected or surprising context	**iii** He is under the affluence of incohol.
4 Comic naming	**D** Misplacing and mixing initial sounds	**iv** She first realised she was turning into a pony when the doctor told her that her throat was a little hoarse.
5 Unorthodox use of words	**E** Funny names for things or characters	**v** I am someone who is permanently pregnant with a play.

Stylistic humour

Stylistic humour makes fun of, or has fun with, language styles.

Activity

Analyse the humour of the following extracts:

From a gravestone in Banbury, Oxfordshire

To the Memory of
Ric:
Richard

Who by gangrene lost first
A Toe afterwards a Leg
& lastly his life
On the 7th day of Aprill 1656

I found Hemlock Jones in the Old Brook Street lodgings, musing before the fire. With the freedom of an old friend I at once threw myself in my usual familiar attitude at his feet, and gently caressed his boot.

'It is raining,' he said, without lifting his head.

'You have been out, then?' I said quickly.

'No. But I see that your umbrella is wet, and that your overcoat has drops of water on it.'

I sat aghast at his penetration. After a pause he said carelessly, as if dismissing the subject: 'Besides, I hear the rain on the window. Listen.'

I listened. I could scarcely credit my ears, but there was the soft pattering of drops on the panes. It was evident that there was no deceiving this man.

From *The Stolen Cigar Case* by Bret Harte, in the style of Conan Doyle's Sherlock Holmes stories

---

Jokes

Why were the early days called the Dark Ages?
Because there were so many knights.

Pupil: Teacher, teacher, my pen's run out.
Teacher: Well run after it then.

What do you call a teacher with chalk dust in her ears?
Anything you want because she can't hear you.

Pupil: What's that fly doing in my soup?
Dinner lady: Looks like crawl.

Graffiti

Xedlysia rules, KO?

Seen in Manchester

Racial prejudice is a pigment of the imagination

Seen in Southampton

French dockers rule Au Quai

Seen in Wolverhampton

YYUR
YYUB
ICUR
YY4Me

Seen in Dukinfield

Activity

Take a familiar writing style or task such as a recipe or newspaper article and apply it to an unexpected topic to make it funny. For example:

Recipe for a terrible job interview.
Newspaper article about an untidy bedroom.

Help ▶▶

Humour in the writing style

Parody	Mocking a style by mimicking it and applying it to ludicrous content.
Irony	Humour that arises when we know that the true meaning of something is the opposite of that given.
Satire	Putting down people or ideas by making them appear ridiculous.

Literary humour

Literary humour makes fun of characters and institutions by exposing their absurdities. Sometimes the humour is gentle, but it can be savage.

Reading a medical encyclopaedia

I idly turned the leaves, and began to indolently study diseases, generally. I forget which was the first distemper I plunged into – some fearful, devastating scourge, I know – and before I had glanced half down the list of 'premonitory symptoms', it was borne in upon me that I had fairly got it.

I sat for a while frozen with horror; and then in the listlessness of despair, I again turned over the pages. I came to typhoid fever – read the symptoms – discovered that I had typhoid fever, must have had it for months without knowing it – wondered what else I had got; turned up St Vitus's Dance – found as I expected, that I had that too – began to get interested in my case, and determined to sift it to the bottom, and so started alphabetically – read up to ague, and learnt that I was sickening for it, and that the acute stage would commence in about another fortnight. Bright's disease, I was relieved to find, I only had in modified form, and so far as that was concerned, I might live for years. Cholera I had, with severe complications; and diphtheria I seemed to have been born with. I plodded conscientiously through the twenty-six letters, and the only malady I could conclude I had not got was housemaid's knee.

From *Three Men in a Boat* by Jerome K. Jerome

Photo of Jerome K. Jerome

Activity

1   Who or what is being mocked?

2   Identify three things about this extract that tell you it is funny rather than serious.

3   To avoid being a one-line joke, how does the writer build the humour over the extract? Look for:
    - his response to each new illness
    - the range and type of illnesses
    - the number and rate of new illnesses he recognises
    - the length and structure of sentences
    - the tone of the narrator.

Read the following extract, which is about the same man.

A visit to Hampton Court Maze

They met some people soon after they had got inside, who said they had been there for three quarters of an hour, and had had enough of it. Harris told them they could follow him if they liked; he was just going in, and then should turn around and come out again. They said it was very kind of him, and followed.

They picked up various other people who wanted to get it over, as they went along, until they absorbed all the persons in the maze. People who had given up all hope of ever getting either in or out, or of ever seeing their home and friends again, plucked up courage at the sight of Harris and his party, and joined the procession, blessing him.

From *Three Men in a Boat* by Jerome K. Jerome

Activity

Write a continuation of the extract in the same style, in which it becomes clear that Harris cannot find the way out and becomes more and more lost. The crowd gradually realise this.

You can read what happens next in Chapter 6 of the novel *Three Men in a Boat* by Jerome K. Jerome.

Hot Tip ▶▶

Gentle literary humour

- The events are funnier for being familiar.
- Readers often laugh at things they do too.
- Gentle humour pokes fun at minor faults, not major sins.
- The focus is often on behaviour and attitudes.
- Vanity, foolishness and selfishness are common themes.

Test it

Your test task is to write a short but funny description in the manner of Jerome K. Jerome about a man who decides to surprise his wife by making dinner for the first time ever. With each stage of the cooking, the dish gets worse and worse.

What you get marks for

Showing a handful of commonplace things that go wrong	2 marks
Exposing the character's over-confidence	2 marks
Building the extract by building up his responses	2 marks
Building up the extract by changing the range or type of events	1 mark
Building up the extract by changing the pace or length of sentences	2 marks
Keeping a deadpan style	1 mark
Total	**10 marks**

ANSWERS

Wordplay

1	B	ii
2	D	iii
3	A	iv
4	E	i
5	C	v

C. HITTING THE RIGHT NOTE

12. The formal voice

In this masterclass you will learn how to:

- write plainly
- write formally
- formalise oral or colloquial language.

Writing plainly

We are lucky to have a well-known writer whose style is considered by everyone to be a good, plain, clear, strong style. The writer is George Orwell who lived between 1903 and 1950. He was both a journalist and a novelist, and he soon developed a style of writing that most people found interesting and easy to follow.

George Orwell wrote *Animal Farm*, *The Road to Wigan Pier* and many other famous novels and articles.

In one of his articles, he gave some good advice about writing plainly. Here are his six guidelines:

Orwell's guidelines

1 Never use a metaphor, simile or other figure of speech which you are used to seeing in print.

2 Never use a long word where a short one will do.

3 If it is possible to cut out a word, always cut it out.

4 Never use the passive where you can use the active.

5 Never use a foreign phrase, a scientific word or a jargon word if you can think of an everyday English equivalent.

6 Break any of these rules sooner than say anything outright barbarous.

From *Politics and the English Language* by George Orwell

Here is a piece of writing to measure against Orwell's guidelines:

Advice to a bride

Keep it constantly in mind, that the happiness of marriage depends entirely on a solid permanent friendship, to which nothing is more opposite than jealousy and distrust. Nor are they less at variance with the true interests of passion. You can never be a gainer by taxing your husband's affection beyond its natural strength; the fear of alarming your jealousy, and bringing on a quarrel, may force him to feign a greater fondness that he feels, but this very effort and constraint will, in fact, diminish, and by degrees extinguish that fondness. There is nothing less likely to increase affection than ill humour and captiousness. The truth is, that pride rather than tenderness usually occasions the unreasonable expectations of an exceptious person, and it is rewarded as it deserves, with mortifications, and the cold dislike of those who suffer it.

From *Letter to a Newly-Married Lady* by Mrs Chapone

Activity

1   How do you rate this extract against Orwell's guidelines?

2   Try writing a cleaner, plainer version of it.

Redrafting
- There's more to redrafting than spelling and punctuation.
- Check for expression and clarity.
- Check for logic and links.
- Leave time after writing so you can return to it with fresh eyes.
- Reading aloud makes it easier to pick out false notes.
- Let someone else read it and comment.
- Use a word processor to save time on revisions.
- If in doubt: simplify, shorten or cut it out.

Moving from talking to writing

Spoken language and written language are expressed differently. Talk is free-flowing and unpunctuated; it shifts around, pauses, repeats, circles round and changes direction mid-sentence. Writing is more measured and formal.

Compare:

Talk
They're, like, friends, they've been, you know, friends for ages. I know people think they're an item but yeah they're just mates – what? – yeah – no, I know – yeah, just mates.

Writing
Despite the rumours Dave and Jez are old friends, not lovers.

Activity

Identify:

- differences in vocabulary and expression
- differences in sentence structure
- why talk and writing produce such different language
- the benefits of talk compared with the benefits of writing.

Writing formally

Formal writing is polite and considerate to the reader you do not know. It is careful to:

- use standard terms and standard grammar they will understand
- avoid expressions they won't know or might cause offence
- be precise and accurate to avoid any misunderstanding
- stay even in tone, and steady in pace, and not get emotional
- be objective, even impersonal, by avoiding 'I'.

Activity

Rewrite the park sign and the letter into polite, positive standard English:

Sign at the park gate

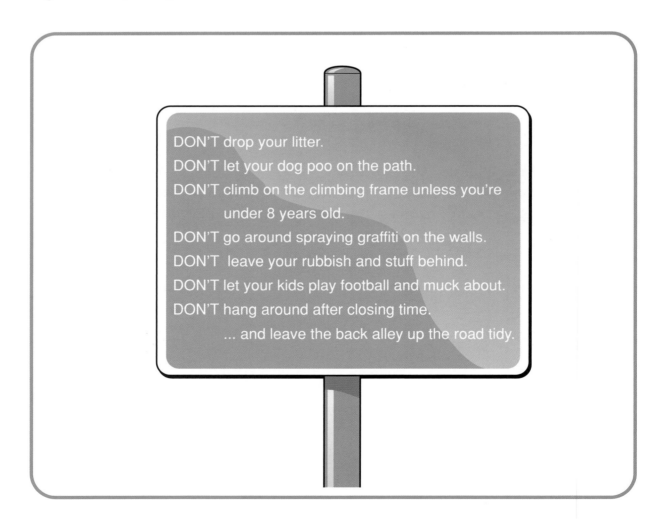

DON'T drop your litter.

DON'T let your dog poo on the path.

DON'T climb on the climbing frame unless you're under 8 years old.

DON'T go around spraying graffiti on the walls.

DON'T leave your rubbish and stuff behind.

DON'T let your kids play football and muck about.

DON'T hang around after closing time.

... and leave the back alley up the road tidy.

Letter of complaint

12 Cedar Road,

Ashton,

Yorkshire

12th May

Dear Mr Knibworth,

I don't mean to complain but the overalls I bought last week turned out to be a nightmare. I'm not saying the material wasn't good stuff like you said, but it's the design that's all wrong. I can't begin to tell you what a pig's ear they've made of the gusset. My hubbie says I look like a penguin, and the neckstrap is killing me. You lot should have fixed it so it fitted. I haven't got £20 to waste, even if you have, so I want my money back, okay?

Yours sincerely,

Janet Hardcastle

>> Test it

Convert this transcript of someone speaking into a formal written statement:

I knew there were summat wrong as soon as a turned off the roundabout 'cos I could see the black car blocking off our road – it was at a funny angle, and the door was open so I knew it wasn't right. Then I turned into the road and I could see this fella outside my house in the street – I thought he was a policeman 'cos he had a dark uniform on and a crash helmet but then I could see it was different – he was a security guard or something. Then I see this other fella on the ground and he's holding his leg and looks terrified and the big guy is shouting and the one on the ground, he's shuffling himself back on the ground – and I thought 'He's going to shoot'. He was shouting his head off and waving his arms around and then – and then – there was this crack – it was *so* loud – I didn't think shots were that loud – louder than on telly – and I see the man on the ground and he's holding his leg and howling like a dog – then the big guy shouts and runs off, right past me in the car. He was a tall bloke – must have been over 6 feet – and fit looking, and white, but I couldn't see his face properly because he had his visor down. Anyway, he gets in the black car and revs it right up and screams off into the London Road. It only took about half a minute. I didn't have time to be frightened, and I went to the man – he was crying but he was alive and he was talking. He had two shots in his left leg, but there was hardly any blood. A neighbour had seen the first shooting and had called the police, and that was when they turned up.

What you get marks for

Reducing it down to the key events and facts	2 marks
Formalising the vocabulary and expression	4 marks
Organising it into clear simple sentences	2 marks
The overall effect is plain, clear and easy to follow	2 marks
Total	**10 marks**

13. Responding in writing

In this masterclass you will learn how to:

- use writing to capture ideas
- annotate a text with first thoughts
- use diagrams and notes to organise ideas.

Using writing to capture ideas

Writing quick notes as you go is a useful way of capturing first impressions and fleeting ideas which are otherwise forgotten. Most writers keep a notebook with them at all times for this purpose.

Writing down a passing idea will help you to articulate it and remember it. This can be useful for:

- planning homework
- collecting ideas before writing
- capturing your response to literature.

Because the notes are for your eyes only, they need not be elaborate, but just enough to jog the memory.

Examples

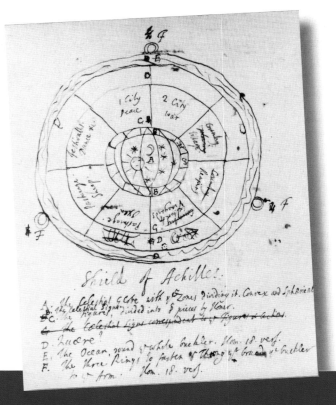

Alexander Pope plans his description of Achilles' shield for his verse translation of Homer's *Iliad*

© **British Library**

Van Gogh's plan for colouring a painting
of fields

© Amsterdam, Van Gogh Museum
(Vincent van Gogh Foundation)

Samuel Johnson's planning notes for
his biography of Alexander Pope, made
in 1780

© British Library

A poet's notebook

This 'notebook' is one of the most important pre-conditions for the composition of the genuine article.

People usually only write about this little book after the poet's death; for years it lies gathering dust, and it's printed posthumously, long after the 'finished' works, but for the writer this book is all-in-all.

Inexperienced poets naturally lack this little book, since they lack practice and experience. Properly worked-out lines are few, and that's why their output is anaemic and tedious.

No beginner will, whatever his talents, write something fine straight off.

From *How are Verses Made?* by Vladimir Mayakovsky

Activity

Gather onto half a sheet of paper a number of ideas and phrases for a poem about either:

Snowfall or **Losing** or **The lost shoe** or **Drowning**

Techniques for generating ideas

- Close your eyes and see it. Describe what you see. Imagine what happens.
- Attend to each of the senses: *sight*, *sound*, *touch*, *taste* and *smell*.
- Notice what you *feel*, what you *think* and what you *remember*.
- Think of it over *time*: past, present, soon, next month, next year, next decade, next century.
- Think of things quite unlike your subject and see if they can be compared, combined or used as a metaphor for an unusual angle on it, e.g. web, fire, tree, knot, birth.

Annotating a text

Here is an example of notes around a speech from *Macbeth*. Macbeth is calling on the night to close in so that he can commit a murder under cover of dark.

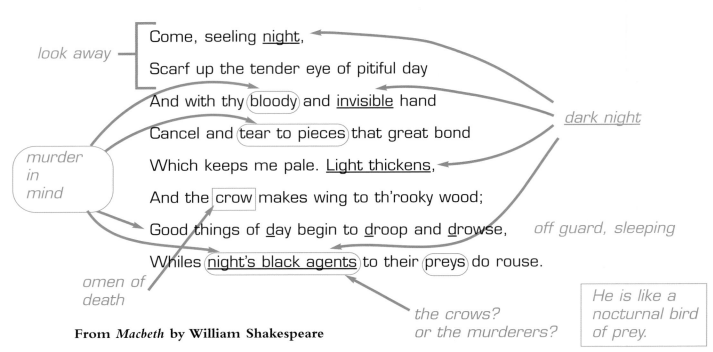

look away

Come, seeling <u>night</u>,

Scarf up the tender eye of pitiful day

And with thy (bloody) and <u>invisible</u> hand

dark night

Cancel and (tear to pieces) that great bond

murder in mind

Which keeps me pale. <u>Light thickens</u>,

And the crow makes wing to th'rooky wood;

Good things of <u>d</u>ay begin to <u>droop</u> and <u>drowse</u>,

off guard, sleeping

Whiles (night's black agents) to their (preys) do rouse.

omen of death

the crows? or the murderers?

He is like a nocturnal bird of prey.

From *Macbeth* by William Shakespeare

Activity

Write out the following lines from *Macbeth* and take five minutes to annotate it in order to understand its meaning and appreciate the use of language. Macbeth is depressed after the death of his wife:

Tomorrow, and tomorrow, and tomorrow
Creeps in this petty pace from day to day
To the last syllable of recorded time;
And all our yesterdays have lighted fools
The way to dusty death. Out, out, brief candle,
Life's but a walking shadow, a poor player
That struts and frets his hour upon the stage
And then is heard no more. It is a tale
Told by an idiot, full of sound and fury
Signifying nothing.

From *Macbeth* by William Shakespeare

Annotation

You can use:

- notes in the margin
- underlining, circling or boxing words
- highlighting in different colours for different questions.

Using diagrams and sketches to organise ideas

You will already know about the use of flow charts, star charts, timelines, columns and grids to plan writing. You can read more about these on page 121 of the section *Notes to the pupil*. The same diagrams are useful for making notes when you research topics or make revision notes.

It is always worth asking yourself how you can arrange your notes so that they are quick, easy and useful for revision. You have to think of the diagram shape that will best fit your topic.

Here is a whole side of writing that has been recorded as a sketch for future revision:

Majorca

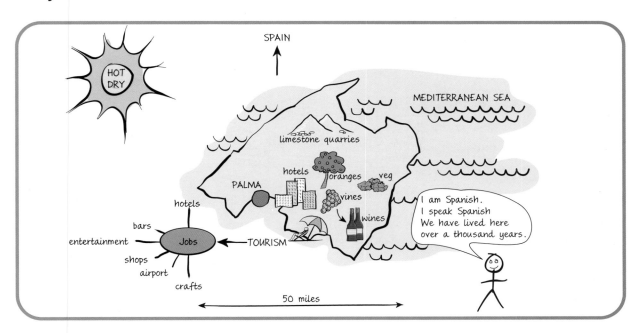

Activity

Say what form you would choose to record:

- A description of the production line in an industrial process.
- An account of the way a baby develops in the womb.
- An explanation of how an orchestra is arranged.
- Five pages of notes about the city of Athens.
- Arguments about the source of crop circles.
- An account of the way the heart works as a pump.
- The properties of the group of gases known as halogens.
- The policies of an American political party.

>> Test it

1   Write out and annotate these lines from Shakespeare in order to understand the meaning and appreciate the language. Macbeth realises that he lacks feelings and is beyond help:

I have almost forgot the taste of fears;
The time has been, my senses would have cooled
To hear a night–shriek and my fell of hair   fell = body hair
Would at a dismal treatise rouse and stir   treatise = story
As life were in it. I have supped full with horrors;
Direness familiar to my slaughterous thoughts
Cannot once start me.   start = startle

From *Macbeth* by William Shakespeare

2   Draw and colour the human snake described in the poem:

She was a Gordian shape of dazzling hue,   Gordian = knotted; hue = colour
Vermilion-spotted, golden, green and blue;
Striped like a zebra, freckled like a pard,   pard = leopard
Eyed like a peacock, and all crimson barr'd;
And full of silver moons
Upon her crest she wore a wannish fire   wannish = pale
Sprinkled with stars, like Ariadne's tiar: tiar = tiara, crown
She had a woman's mouth with all its pearls complete:
And for her eyes: what could such eyes do there
But weep, and weep, that they were born so fair?

From *Lamia* by John Keats

What you get marks for

Picking out words that express Macbeth's hardness and his bloodiness	2 marks
Picking out two places where he expresses world-weariness	1 mark
Understanding the gist of the *Macbeth* speech	1 mark
Including at least six colours in the right places on the snake	2 marks
Getting the body, head, eyes and teeth right	2 marks
Getting the spot, stripes, bars and stars right	2 marks
Total	**10 marks**

14. Making comparisons

In this masterclass you will learn how to:

- express comparisons and contrasts
- identify significant points of comparison
- structure comparative writing.

Comparing and contrasting

People often ask for comparisons when what they really want you to do is to compare *and* contrast. This means seeing how they are alike and how they differ. A common fault in comparisons is forgetting to compare because the contrasts are so interesting.

It helps if you have a range of useful words and phrases for moving between the two things you compare. It also avoids repetition.

Activity

1   Spend one minute discussing each of these comparisons, but stay alert to the kind of words you use to express the differences and similarities:
    - Compare a brother and sister you know.
    - Compare primary school and secondary school.
    - Compare the lifestyle of girls and boys.

2   Reflect on the words you used in moving between one thing and the other.
    e.g. *On the other hand…* List them.

3   Separate your list into words that compare and words that contrast ideas.

4   Check your answers against the list on the next page.

Hot Tip

Making comparisons

- Have a list of handy words and phrases ready to use.
- You will always find interesting differences, but don't forget the obvious similarities.
- Vary the way you make the comparisons. The expression *X is this*, but *Y is that* is fine in speech but sounds repetitious in writing.
- Be aware that some comparisons are more significant than others. Group your ideas around the big important points.

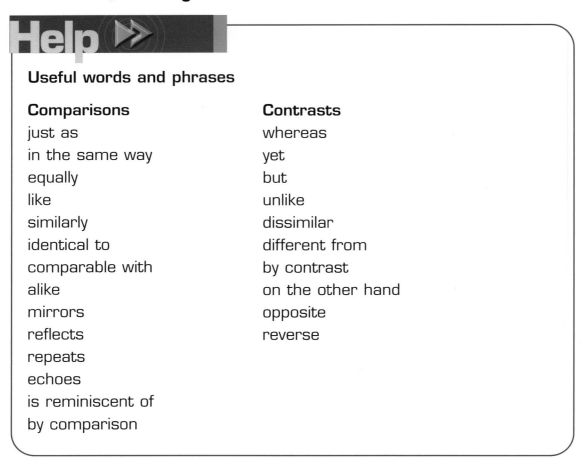

Help ▷▷

Useful words and phrases

Comparisons	Contrasts
just as	whereas
in the same way	yet
equally	but
like	unlike
similarly	dissimilar
identical to	different from
comparable with	by contrast
alike	on the other hand
mirrors	opposite
reflects	reverse
repeats	
echoes	
is reminiscent of	
by comparison	

Constructing comparisons

The easiest structure for comparing and contrasting is as follows:

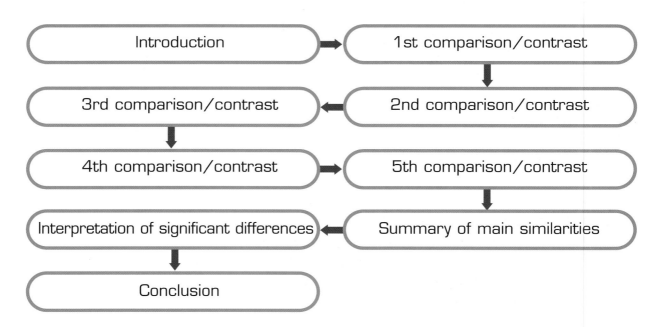

Introduction → 1st comparison/contrast

3rd comparison/contrast ← 2nd comparison/contrast

4th comparison/contrast → 5th comparison/contrast

Interpretation of significant differences ← Summary of main similarities

Conclusion

Activity

Finding the main points

This is a discussion task.

1 Spend ten minutes discussing the similarities and differences between two television soap operas (e.g. *Eastenders* and *Coronation Street*) or two reality television shows (e.g. *Big Brother* and *I'm a Celebrity, Get Me Out of Here*).

2 Make two lists – *Similarities* and *Differences*.

3 Pick out – or summarise – the two most important similarities and the two most significant differences.

4 Consider how you distinguished the important points from the minor points.

5 Are there any points you can roll together and re-express as one big point?

6 Prepare a writing plan for this comparison, based on the sequence opposite.

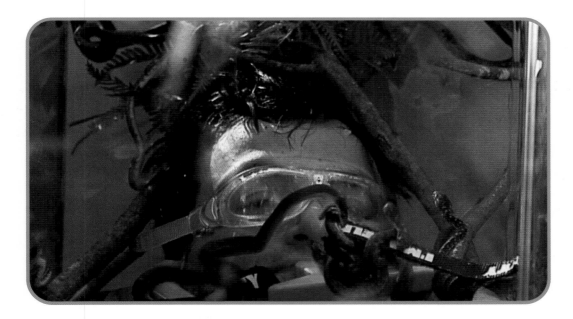

Hot Tip ▶▶

Finding the main points

Go beyond obvious surface features to get to the heart of the matter. Look for the most fundamental points, the 'family' likeness and the root cause of the differences.

- The main points are **less likely** to be about appearance, presentation, subject matter, behaviour or personalities.
- They are **more likely** to be about purpose, beliefs, themes, motives and human interest.

Drawing out significance

The best writing goes beyond making the main points and tries to explain them. This means seeing *why* things are similar and explaining *why* they are different. It helps the reader to understand why some differences don't matter but others are significant.

Activity

- Discuss the similarities and differences between two political parties, two religions, or two periods in history.
- After listing some of the obvious similarities and differences, try to explain what lies at the root of the differences.

Activity

Read the example opposite:

- What are the main points of comparison that are made?
- How does the writer try to explain their significance?

A writing frame for a comparison

- X and Y share common…
- They are both…
- They are also similar in…
- It is well-known that they both…
- The main differences lie in…
- Where X does *this*…, Y does *that*…
- X is often…, whereas Y is inclined to…
- X is…, Y on the other hand is…
- Behind these differences lies a more significant *contrast/clash/ disagreement/fault line* which is…
- This explains why…
- Overall, one can see how both X and Y are… but they remain divided by…

This writing frame can and should be adapted to suit your topic and line of thought. Change it to suit.

Example

Here is a piece of comparative writing. It is a newspaper review of a Joan Baez concert. The writer recalls attending the same concert 50 years ago.

I was apprehensive about hearing her again, live, with a band to back her but no studio technicians to protect her.

I need not have worried. The sweet voice is not quite as effortless as it was, but it is richer and more lived in, like her face. Though her hair is grey now and cut short, there is still a kind of youthful lightness about her slight figure, fine-boned face and casual, rather dowdy clothes that seem to have nothing to do with showbiz or glamour. Even after all these years on the circuit, her voice still sounds as natural as birdsong.

Halfway through the evening, the band slipped quietly away, leaving Baez perched on a high stool, alone with her guitar, singing the songs that had made her famous – songs like *Fare thee well* and *The night they drove old Dixie down* – her pure and plaintive voice as effortless as ever.

The audience was made up mostly of people of Baez's age and, unlike Baez, they looked it: white-haired, grey-faced, overweight couples in their sixties, some of them with their grandchildren in tow. But under her spell they had got their youth back and they wouldn't let go. I lost count of the number of encores she sang, but the evening did not end until she pointedly signed off with *May you stay forever young*.

She herself has stayed magically young.

By Al Alvarez in the *Observer* newspaper, 8 February 2004

Activity

Write up the conclusion to one of the comparisons you have discussed in this unit. Explain the underlying reasons for the similarities and differences you found.

>> Test it

Compare:

either

your relationship with two relatives (e.g. mother and father, sister and brother, sets of grandparents)

or

two similar events such as two concerts or two weddings.

What you get marks for

Organising the writing into clear paragraphs	1 mark
Remembering to say how the two cases are similar	1 mark
Organising the writing around key comparisons	2 marks
Using a variety of expressions to make the comparisons	2 marks
Attempting to explain the root cause of the differences	2 marks
Getting to the heart of the matter	2 marks
Total	**10 marks**

15. Tailoring text

In this masterclass you will learn how to:

- adapt writing to the needs of its readers
- ensure that writing is fit for its purpose
- edit writing to the length required.

Writing that is suitable for its readers

In adapting writing for a different readership, you should consider:

- the relevance of the **content**
- the level of **difficulty** it poses
- the **suitability** of the language
- anything that may cause **offence**

and decide what to leave in, cut out or revise.

Consider this information taken from a medical encyclopaedia:

What is sneezing?

The involuntary, convulsive expulsion of air through the nose and mouth as a result of irritation of the upper respiratory tract. The irritation may be caused by inflammation of the tract, which occurs in the common cold, influenza, and allergic rhinitis (hay fever); by the presence of mucus; or by inhaling an irritant substance such as dust or pepper.

From the *BMA Family Health Encyclopaedia*

Activity

- Discuss the changes that would be necessary if you were asked to adapt this text for use with nine-year-olds.
- Rewrite it.

Nearly everything that is written is drafted first. Many pieces of writing start life as ideas, notes, emails or plans. At a certain point, they are rewritten with their audience in mind.

Read this email sequence about planning a concert. Remember that email sequences start with the most recent entry and work back.

To: Ed Faceman
From: Lin Gapp
Re: Concert
Date: Thursday 14:10

I've just confirmed with the venue that we start at 8, so we open doors at 7.15, I think.
Bar is open throughout. No meals. Crisps, etc are available.
No cloakroom, alas.
That seems to be it. Will you knock up a poster?

To: Lin Gapp
From: Rea Demartez (Haringey Palace)
Re: 6 June event
Date: Thursday 13:35

Sorry, no cloakroom, but the bar is open to the public from 5pm, though we don't usually open the concert hall itself until 45 minutes before the first band start. 8pm start is fine with me.

To: Rea Demartez (Haringey Palace)
From: Lin Gapp
Re: 6 June event
Date: Thursday 12:05

Good. We'll get going with the tickets and posters right away.
The warm up band is available from 8, and the main band not before 9.
What are the arrangements about the bar?
Do they take coats in with them or is there a cloakroom?

To: Lin Gapp
From: Rea Demartez (Haringey Palace)
Re: 6 June event
Date: Thursday 8:55

Everything is go at this end.
How many bands and what time do they start?
As soon as I receive the printed tickets I'll open the ticket hotline which will be 0800 1111 234.

To: Ed Faceman
From: Lin Gapp
Re: Concert
Date: Wednesday 15:20

The main band is The Squash. They're Irish rock, 4 guys. They do two sets of 45 mins each.

They've had two chart hits – you may remember 'Before sunset' and 'Birmingham Blues'. I think a lot of their fans are a bit older – 20s, early 30s.

The warm up act is The Three Sisters. They're real triplets! They do ballads and swing and their big thing is that they don't have instruments. Like a barber's quartet, they use their voices for instrumental backing. Quite strange but good.

We have publicity photos you could use.

We're charging £15 a ticket, with a reduction to £10 for under 18s, students, over 60s (don't expect many of them!) and parties of more than 10.

To: Lin Gapp
From: Ed Faceman
Re: Concert
Date: Tuesday 11:45

I don't know them – can you give me a feel for the kind of music and target audience?

To: Ed Faceman
From: Lin Gapp
Re: Concert
Date: Tuesday 9:30

Great to hear from you…. Thanks!
It's The Squash, with The Three Sisters as back up. Do you know them?
The venue is The Haringey Palace.
It's a Friday evening – 6th June.

To: Lin Gapp
From: Ed Faceman
Re: Concert
Date: Monday 13:55

Hi Lin
Yes, sure, if we keep it simple we can do you something over next weekend. Is that soon enough? Give us the details – who it is, back up group, style, time, etc.

To: Ed Faceman
From: Lin Gapp
Re: Concert
Date: Monday 11:25

Ed,
I have a rush job. I need 6,000 posters for a concert we're putting together at high speed at a London venue. Can you help?

Activity

Use the information contained in the emails to design a poster for the target audience.

Writing that is fit for purpose

To adapt writing for a different purpose, you should consider:

- whether the **form** it takes is right for the new job
- whether the **style of language** is suitable for it
- whether it should be changed in **the way it addresses its readers**.

How do you know, for example, that a note to the milkman should be short, polite and in note form?

Number 12 Brick Street

Please cancel milk this Wed and Thurs.

3 extra pints on Friday, please.

Thanks!

You may just be copying what you have seen others do, but there are good reasons why this particular style works. Think about it. Why short? Why polite? Why in note form?

Activity

Discuss what form and style these writing tasks should take, and why:

- Directions for walking to your cousin's house about a mile away.
- A few words written in a card to a relative after the death of a loved one.
- An email to a friend explaining why you didn't turn up to an agreed meeting.
- A letter of apology to the school caretaker, who is off work this week after twisting his ankle falling over your school bag which had been left just outside his door.

Tailoring writing to the length required

- Sometimes you will need to reduce writing to make it fit in a particular space or if there is a limit on the number of words allowed.

Activity

Here is a real article from television listings. Suppose the editor asks you to cut it from 78 words to 45 exactly. Discuss what you would cut or summarise and why, and how you would close the gap by re-expressing sentences.

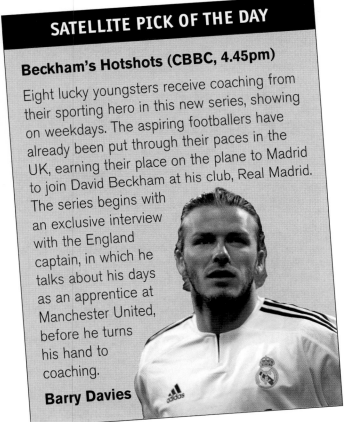

SATELLITE PICK OF THE DAY

Beckham's Hotshots (CBBC, 4.45pm)

Eight lucky youngsters receive coaching from their sporting hero in this new series, showing on weekdays. The aspiring footballers have already been put through their paces in the UK, earning their place on the plane to Madrid to join David Beckham at his club, Real Madrid.

The series begins with an exclusive interview with the England captain, in which he talks about his days as an apprentice at Manchester United, before he turns his hand to coaching.

Barry Davies

Help ▶▶

Editing down

The most common cuts are:

- the least important parts
- the dull or repetitious parts
- the parts that can be summarised or shortened most easily
- the details, examples or quotations.

>> Test it

Your test task is to convert this article, which appeared on the front page of a national newspaper, into an informative article for the school magazine, at about a third of its current length.

Random drugs tests for pupils

Schoolchildren will be subjected to random drug testing, the government announced yesterday, under new guidance for headteachers to be published shortly.

The move, routine in some American schools, is designed to reassure parents worried about increasing availability of drugs in the playground.

But it raises serious questions over the invasion of pupils' civil liberties: random testing has not been introduced in workplaces because to take samples without consent from an adult constitutes assault.

Drug testing will not be compulsory for schools, but new guidance for headteachers next month will advise on how to start a programme if they wish.

'If heads believe they have a problem in their school then they should be able to do random drug testing,' said a spokesman.

Heads who want to introduce it will have to gain the 'appropriate' consent from either the parents or the pupil, probably depending on the child's age. The move will not require a change in law.

Those who test positive are expected to be offered treatment rather than be expelled.

The announcement is reminiscent of previous headline-grabbing initiatives generated during times of crisis. But a survey earlier this month suggested almost two-thirds of British parents would support random testing. Several private schools already use it.

From the *Observer* newspaper, 22 February 2004

What you get marks for

Shortening it to about a third of its length	3 marks
Keeping in the main information	2 marks
Expressing it in language most pupils will understand	2 marks
Not going 'over the top' or exaggerating	1 mark
Finding an angle that will interest most pupils	2 marks
Total	**10 marks**

16. Synthesising text

In this masterclass you will learn how to:

- assemble information from different sources
- find a line to take through several ideas
- flesh out ideas in prose.

Assembling information from different sources

Writers often need to draw together information from very different sources. The writer's job is to pull it all together into a coherent whole.

1   A sensible first step is to read it all to **get a feel** for the topic.
2   Then, **start with a framework** for your finished piece, and slot the information into that. It makes for smoother, integrated writing. For example:

Example

A CAREER IN THE MEDIA – careers advice		
Section	**Main points**	**Source**
Advantages	Growing industry Career prospects Good pay (in time)	Careers handbook page 121 BBC recruitment pages 3–5
Disadvantages	Low pay at start Long hours Mainly freelance	Interview John and Jamil Careers handbook page 122
Television	Rapidly changing Need qualifications Many technical jobs	BBC recruitment pages 1–10 College courses
Publishing	Varied work, e.g. writing, printing Local and national press Magazines and books	Newspaper websites University journalism courses
Other jobs	Web design and editing Advertising Radio	Media textbook pages 42–6 Careers handbook pages 24, 56 Interview Jamil
Conclusion	Can be exciting, well-paid at top	Long hours, low pay to start, technology changing rapidly

Suppose you are planning to write a short article for a local magazine on flesh-eating plants. You have:

- an account on the Internet about a man who claims to have been bitten by a swaying red creeper in the Amazon jungle
- a plant shop list of six types of carnivorous plants they stock including Latin names, growing conditions, cost, size, pictures and feeding instructions
- detailed information about the Venus Fly Trap plant aimed at younger children, explaining how it catches and digests flies
- an entry in an encyclopaedia which gives information about where carnivorous plants grow in the wild and how they catch and digest animals
- an entry from a more detailed encyclopaedia which also includes information about the first examples ever found and recorded
- your sister, who keeps them.

Activity

You have plenty of information, but how will you stitch it together into an article that other people will want to read?

Imagine the finished article, then decide on sub-headings to go in the left-hand column of your planning grid.

Finding a line to take

Writing about events is easy because you can follow the chronological sequence. With information, argument, discussion or critical writing the main task is to find an organising principle for your writing. Some common organising principles are:

- order of importance, e.g. putting your most persuasive reasons first
- order of interest, e.g. putting the most fascinating details first
- alphabetical order, e.g. a glossary or an A-Z of your subject.

But sometimes it's not so obvious. A good tip is to list four or five aims for your piece of writing. These are the things you want your reader to get out of reading it.

Suppose you want to cover all the things you need to know about GCSEs if you arrive in England in Year 9, and have to choose next year's subjects.

The aims of this piece of writing are to help the reader:

- to understand what GCSEs are
- to know what is involved in studying GCSE and sitting the examination
- to explain how many you can do and how you choose them
- to understand what to do next to make the choice.

These aims could be used as the organising plan:

INTRODUCING GCSEs		
Section	**Main points**	**Source**
What GCSEs are	Usually 2 year course Usually age 14–16 Coursework, exams in June Grades	School options booklet AQA website Timetable
What is involved in studying and sitting the exam	3 hours a week each subject Homework twice a week The syllabus Mocks in January Essays Study leave	History syllabus Homework timetable School calendar
How many you can do and how to choose	Compulsory subjects Option blocks Balance of subjects Career needs	School options booklet
What to do next to make a choice	Talk to teachers and parents Select from option blocks Hand in to Mr Blean by half term	Option form

Activity

1 An autobiography often works in chronological order, moving from childhood to the present day. Think creatively. Are there other ways to organise an autobiography?

2 Think of a way of organising the content of an article for the Residents' Association newsletter about an accident black spot on a local road.

3 The headteacher has asked the school council of pupils to suggest improvements to the areas where pupils spend time out of class, such as the fields, playgrounds and seating areas. However, opinion is very divided. Quite a few people want more benches, new tables and extra seating, but others want sports equipment, rain shelters, drinks machines, pitches marked out, a TV room, easy chairs, a tuck shop, a common room, a place to make hot drinks, gardens, flowerbeds, swings, and much more. Apart from more seating, there were no other clear favourites. How will you write up your findings to represent the spread of opinion?

Fleshing out ideas

Once you have the ideas in place, you will want to add examples, details and comments. But the biggest challenge is to find the form of words that will bring it all together. A good way to start is to write the opening words of each section so that you have a writing frame to guide you when you come to write. For example:

A CAREER IN THE MEDIA – careers advice		
Section	**Main points**	**Opening line**
Advantages	Growing industry Career prospects Good pay (in time)	Have you ever considered a career in the media? A job in TV or publishing can be rewarding because…
Disadvantages	Low pay at start Long hours Mainly freelance	That's not to say it's an easy walk to high pay and fame. On the contrary…
Television	Rapidly changing Need qualifications Many technical jobs	Television attracts many young people with talents in acting, writing…
Publishing	Varied work, e.g. writing, printing Local and national press Magazines and books	Publishing may be less glamorous, but it is certainly…
Other jobs	Web design and editing Advertising Radio	There are a plethora of interesting careers in other media including…
Conclusion	Can be exciting, well-paid at top but long hours, low pay to start, technology changing rapidly	A career in the media may be the path for you if you are prepared to…

Writing section starters

- Start with something that grabs the reader's attention.
- Avoid listing, e.g. *My first point is…*
- Vary the sentence structure.
- Choose wording that will lead you into your main point.

Activity

Write section starters for the Introducing GCSEs plan.

Test it

Your test task is to assemble a table of headings, main points and section starters for an article on Daredevils.

What you get marks for

Assembling a list of headings that sound positively interesting	2 marks
Assembling the headings in a sensible clear order	1 mark
Listing at least three main points under each heading	3 marks
Writing at least four interesting section starters which will make people want to read on	4 marks
Total	**10 marks**

E. WRITING FOR THE TEST

17. Critical tools

In this masterclass you will learn how to:

- define key literary terms
- spell key literary terms
- check a piece of writing for its literary qualities.

Defining key literary terms

Activity

Match the terms to the correct definitions:

Terms	Definition
alliteration	When a word sounds like the thing it describes
onomatopoeia	An overtone or feeling associated with a word
symbol	Compares one thing with something else
assonance	Compares one thing in terms of another
metaphor	A sound in one word is repeated in others for effect
connotation	A feeling of completeness when things are resolved at the end of a story
simile	Giving the words straight from the text
allusion	Refers to something outside the text and assumes the reader will know about it
image	A thing that stands for or represents something bigger
quotation	A time, place or experience is recreated
closure	The first sound in a word is repeated in others for effect
evocation	A picture which is brought to mind

Take turns to test each other on the meanings of the terms or, vice-versa, the terms that go with a definition.

Spelling key terms

1 Words within words

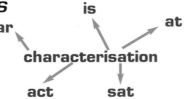

char   is   at

characterisation

act   sat

Activity: Word-spotting

How many ready-made words can you find inside these words? Look for words of two letters or more.

onomatopoeia	**dialogue**
alliteration	**metaphor**
theatrical	**atmosphere**

Find the answers at the end of this masterclass.

2 Mnemonics

Rhythm

Helps

Your

Two

Hips

Move

Activity: DIY mnemonics

Make up mnemonics for:

rhyme   **soliloquy**   **simile**   **audience**

neCeSSary

1 collar

2 sleeves

Mnemonics

- Use each letter as the initial sound of the words in a sentence.
- Make a phrase that uses the word and the word within it, e.g. bu**sin**ess is a sin; I be**lie**ved the lie.
- Find a way to remember the tricky bit of the word, e.g. one **C**ollar, two **S**leeves in ne**cess**ary.
- Colour over or illustrate the difficult bit of a word.

3 Cryptic clues

Activity: Puzzle

Work out these five literary terms using the clues:

* Inside this storyteller, there's a rodent and a rocky hilltop.
* He sees himself as old father time.
* I go to buy a harp: the life story of a Welsh wonder.
* Viewers were mortified.
* Make an effort to find what else this American novelist wrote.

Find the answers at the end of this masterclass.

Make up your own cryptic clues for:

repetition   **connotation**   **author**

4 Say the word as it is spelt

Remember the silent letter by saying it out loud when you speak the word. Try these:

s<u>c</u>ene   **play<u>w</u>right**   **dis<u>c</u>ipline**

5 Link two words that are related in meaning and spelling

Author ⟶ authority, authorise, authenticity (auth = I say so)

Activity: Related words

Find relatives for these words and explain the link in meaning:

imagery   **scene**   **playwright**
tension   **simile**   **audience**

Find the answers at the end of this masterclass.

Activity: Learning spellings

Learn the spellings given on this page and take turns to test each other.

Roots
Family words share a common root, often coming from the old Latin or Greek words. This example is from old Greek:
Auto = self
Bio = life ⎫
Graph = written ⎭   autobiography

Literary qualities

Whenever you write about the style and quality of a piece of writing, always comment about the effect first. Then talk about how it was cleverly created by using certain techniques. This will stop you making a common mistake which is spotting a technique and then forgetting to say how and why it is used.

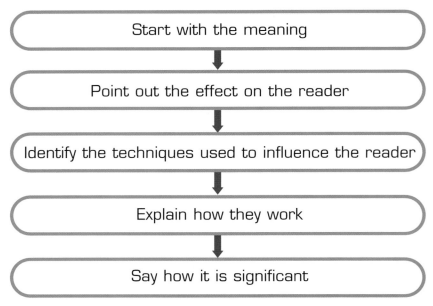

Start with the meaning

↓

Point out the effect on the reader

↓

Identify the techniques used to influence the reader

↓

Explain how they work

↓

Say how it is significant

Example

> ### Vertigo (a fear of heights)
>
> With a lurch like a vomit he remembered where he was. There was a lost pulsing ache in the soles of his feet, and a hot weakness around his ankles and knees. There was a dangerous lightness in his head now, as if it was floating away, weightless. The tower appeared to be swaying.
>
> From *The Idea of Perfection* by Kate Grenville

Commentary:

The narrator describes the sensation of vertigo experienced by the character. Nausea is conveyed in the choice of words 'vomit', 'hot', 'lightness in the head' and 'swaying' but there is also a sense of danger that he is unsteady and might fall in the words 'lurch', 'lost', 'dangerous', 'floating away' and 'weightless'. The first sentence tells us what he is doing but in the later sentences, he is inactive and his sensations have taken over as the subject of the sentences. The reader experiences his sickness but recognises the danger he is in.

Activity: Check the steps

Check this commentary against the steps above. Are they all there?

Checklist of literary effects

Words

Choice

Repetition

Patterns

Bias

Connotations

Imagery

Visual images

Appeals to the senses

Details mentioned

Metaphors

Similes

Sound effects

Onomatopoeia

Alliteration

Rhyme

Rhythm

Pace

Sounds like...

Expression

Narrator

Tone

Formality

Sentences

Structure

Length

Active/passive

Verbs

Structure and organisation

Sequence

Chunking

Focuses

Layout

Help ≫

From these six headings, learn a mnemonic – WISE SS or E-SWISS – and write the six headings on your paper at the start of examinations. Use it as a checklist.

⟫ Test it ⟩⟩⟩

1   Spell the words on page 97, when they are read aloud to you.

2   Remember the mnemonic for the literary checklist and three items in each category.

3   Write one paragraph about the state of mind of this man with vertigo:

> Now he was sweaty and dizzy, and hot and cold at once. He must not move. Whatever happened, he must not move. He must go on hanging onto this piece of gritty pipe. He must keep his feet just exactly where they were. If he kept them locked on to this plank, he would not spin away into space. He heard someone moan. It could have been himself.

From *The Idea of Perfection* by Kate Grenville

What you get marks for

Start with two marks and lose half a mark for every misspelt word   2 marks

Half a mark for each category completed   3 marks

One mark for each step completed:
- Start with the meaning
- Point out the effect on the reader
- Identify the techniques used to influence the reader
- Explain how they work
- Say how it is significant   5 marks

Total   **10 marks**

ANSWERS

Words within words

Onomatopoeia (6) on, no, mat, at, to, top

Alliteration (10) all, lit, iteration, era, rat, at, ration, ratio, ion, on

Theatrical – (5) the, he, heat, eat, at

Dialogue – (2) dial, log

Metaphor – (3) me, met, tap

Atmosphere – (5) at, sphere, here, he, her

Cryptic clues

Narrator

Image

Autobiography

Audience

Poetry

Related words

Imagery – imagine, imaginary, imagination (image = visualise)

Tension – tense, intensity (tense = wound up tight)

Scene – scenic, scenario (scen = view)

Simile – similar, verisimilitude, assimilate, simulation (simil = alike)

Playwright – cartwright, wheelwright (wright = make)

Audience – auditorium, audible (audi = hear)

18. *Quoting and referring*

In this masterclass you will learn how to:

- use quotation
- refer back to the text
- integrate quotation and reference into your writing.

When you write about literature and the media, you will often refer back to things that happened or were said in the text. In critical writing, the words used can be cited as evidence or by way of example.

Quoting the text

Quote an extract from the text if:

- it sums up a point better than you can
- it speaks for itself
- it isn't over-long.

Example

Doug is both selfish and cunning:

'Doug only gave when it was in his interests to do so. All his gifts came with strings attached, and he expected to cash in his acts of generosity.'

Even family gifts were given with an ulterior motive of increasing their productivity.

Quoting

To quote:

- lead into a quote with a short sentence to get the reader ready
- leave a line before and after the quote
- indent the quotation
- wrap the quotation in speech marks
- follow through with an example or comment.

Quoting as you go

Often it is more effective if you quote the text by weaving words and phrases into your own sentences. It shows that you have paid close attention to the evidence in the text.

Quote as you go if:

- the quotation is pithy and apt
- the wording is significant
- the turn of phrase is better than yours
- you can find a way to fit it into your sentence.

Example

Doug is described by the office manager as 'mean-spirited' and by Bessie as a 'cold fish'. He deceives his sisters with 'calculated half-truths' that he tells himself are protective but in reality are designed to avoid debate.

Quoting as you go

- Keep the quotations short.
- Put quotation marks around the words lifted from the text.
- Weave them into the wording of the sentence.
- You still need to draw out any points you want to make about the quotations.
- The trick is to get the wording of the sentence right for slotting them in.

Referring to the text

Referring to the text means pointing out evidence in your own words.

Example

Doug's selfishness is revealed in the way he holds back money and important information from his sisters. Even when he presents each of them with a computer for Christmas, his real motive is to increase their working hours and profitability.

Referring to the text

Refer to the text if:

- it's easier to make the point in your own words
- the section you refer to is too long to quote
- the actual words are not significant.

Activity: Quoting

Consider each of the following situations. Which would be best:

- to refer?
- to quote a short extract?
- to quote as you go?

A To sum up the main reasons for the downfall of a character.

B To expose prejudice in the choice of language.

C To identify the turning point in a play when the main character realises he is wrong.

D To discuss the shock effect of the opening line of a novel.

E To explain how a leaflet about cruelty to animals engages the sympathy of the reader.

Choosing between referring, quoting an extract or quoting as you go

There are no hard and fast rules. A lot depends on what quotations are available in the text. However, it may be useful to:

- **refer** if the focus is on events, plot, motives, abstract ideas or summing up
- **quote a short extract** if it is good enough and important enough to merit a whole section of its own
- **quote as you go** if the focus is on choice of language, detail or literary technique.

F To compare the behaviour of two characters.

G To explore how a poet has created a mood of menacing silence.

H To draw links between a real person and a character in a play.

I To explain why the hero of a novel decides to join the army.

After completing the activity, find the answers at the end of this masterclass.

Integrating quotation, reference and comment

As you have seen, a common way of quoting evidence is to:

> Make your point

> Provide example(s) as evidence

> Draw out the significance

In this extract, the writer is describing the canals of Venice. She uses a number of words and expressions that give the place a sinister feel.

The canal was narrow, the houses on either side seemed to close in upon it, and in the daytime, with the sun's reflection on the water and the windows of the houses open, bedding upon the balconies, a canary singing in a cage, there had been an impression of warmth, of secluded shelter. Now, ill-lit, almost in darkness, the windows of the houses shuttered, the water dank, the scene appeared altogether different, neglected, poor, and the long narrow boats moored to the slippery steps of cellar entrances looked like coffins.

From *Don't Look Now* by Daphne du Maurier

Activity: Finding quotations

- Find **two** examples of sinister images.
- Find **four** examples of the writer appealing to different senses (sight, smell, hearing and feeling).
- Find **three** striking examples of individual words chosen to give a sinister feel.
- Use the sequence at the top of the opposite page to write a paragraph in which you show how the sinister atmosphere has been created.

Leading into quotations

The knack of quoting is to write a sentence that leads naturally into the quotation. Here are two forms of wording that you can use or adapt:

The writer creates an impression of... by...
A strong sense of... is suggested by...

It is useful to have a range of different expressions such as:

The writer creates an impression of...
The writer conveys a sense of...
The writer portrays...
The writer conjures up a...
The writer evokes feelings of...
The writer paints a picture that is full of...
The writer implies that...
The writer suggests that...

The description is charged with...
The description is imbued with...
The description is loaded with...
The description is full of...
The description is rich in...

Always read back what you write to check that it sounds natural.

≫ Test it ⟩⟩⟩

Your test task is to write a paragraph in which you explain, using quotation, how the writer has created a feeling of desolation in this description of a wasteland:

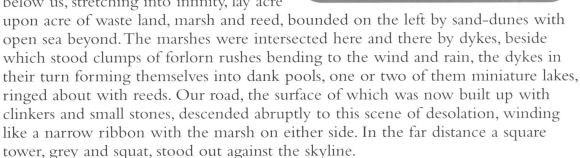

Wasteland

The sandy track topped a rise and there below us, stretching into infinity, lay acre upon acre of waste land, marsh and reed, bounded on the left by sand-dunes with open sea beyond. The marshes were intersected here and there by dykes, beside which stood clumps of forlorn rushes bending to the wind and rain, the dykes in their turn forming themselves into dank pools, one or two of them miniature lakes, ringed about with reeds. Our road, the surface of which was now built up with clinkers and small stones, descended abruptly to this scene of desolation, winding like a narrow ribbon with the marsh on either side. In the far distance a square tower, grey and squat, stood out against the skyline.

From *The Breakthrough* by Daphne du Maurier

What you get marks for

Finding suitable words and phrases to quote	2 marks
Using quotation marks in the right places	1 mark
Weaving the quotes elegantly into your sentences	4 marks
Drawing out the main point(s) in your own words	3 marks
Total	**10 marks**

ANSWERS

Refer, quote an extract or quote as you go

Remember there are no hard and fast rules, but these are the answers you might think of first:

A Refer   **F** Refer

B Quote as you go   **G** Quote as you go

C Quote a short extract   **H** Refer

D Quote a short extract   **I** Refer

E Quote as you go

19. Explaining effects

In this masterclass you will learn how to:

- identify a literary effect
- explain a literary effect
- offer an interpretation.

You will need to refer to the list of skills on page 101. It lists literary effects under six headings:

Words

Imagery

Sound effects

Expression

Sentences

Structure and organisation

The list is in no special order, and every text is different. Only a few of the items will be relevant to one text and the importance of each item will vary from text to text. Use the list to check that you've looked for everything, but **don't** use it as a way to structure your writing. That must be based on the answers to the question.

Step 1: Read the text

The train bore me away, through the monstrous scenery of slag-heaps, chimneys, piled scrap-iron, foul canals, paths of cindery mud criss-crossed by the print of clogs. This was March but the weather had been horribly cold and everywhere there were mounds of blackened snow. As we moved slowly through the outskirts of town we passed row after row of little grey slum houses running at right angles to the embankment.

From *The Road to Wigan Pier* by George Orwell

Step 2: Pinpoint your own first responses to the question

What impression of the city is given by the writer?

> Industrial wasteland
>
> Scene from the 1930s/40s – clogs, slums
>
> Poverty
>
> Bleak, cold, grimy, ugly

Step 3: Find the main details that gave you that impression

The train bore me away, through the <u>monstrous scenery of slag-heaps, chimneys, piled scrap-iron, foul canals, paths of cindery mud</u> criss-crossed by the print of <u>clogs</u>. This was March but the weather had been <u>horribly cold</u> and everywhere there were mounds of blackened <u>snow</u>. As we moved slowly through the outskirts of town we passed <u>row after row of little grey slum houses</u> running at right angles to the embankment.

Trust your first impressions because they take you to the big obvious points.

Step 4: Use the checklist to scan for other points

> Words – monstrous, foul – negative
>
> Imagery – cold colours (blackened snow, grey), grim industrial images (slag-heaps, canal, cindery mud)
>
> Sound effects – slow, long sentences
>
> Expression – negative adjectives on most nouns
>
> Sentences – use lists to pile on the grim sights
>
> Structure and organisation – train moving past the sights (bore me – moved slowly – passed) we are seeing the scenery moving past his carriage window.

Step 5: Start with a phrase that makes you answer the question

> The writer has painted a picture of a city which is...
>
> The city is depicted as...
>
> The reader is given an impression of a city that is...

Step 6: Complete it with a summing up

> The writer presents the city as a bleak, inhospitable and ugly industrial wasteland.

Notice how compact this sentence is. It tells you four important things about the impression.

Step 7: Point out two or three ways in which the effect has been achieved, quoting by way of evidence and example

This is where you point out the techniques used and quote them as evidence.

> Ugly images of the landscape are piled one on top of the other in a list:
>
> 'slag-heaps, chimneys, piled scrap-iron, foul canals, paths of cindery mud'
>
> and the adjectives are charged with negative feeling: 'monstrous', 'foul'. The bleakness of the scene is increased by the visual imagery: 'blackened snow' and 'grey houses'. Even the weather is 'horribly cold'.

Step 8: Draw out how the effect works

Pull back a little from the detail and explain the writer's strategy for influencing the reader.

> A string of small, depressing details recreates the scenes that pass before the narrator's eyes as he looks from the carriage window. They roll by, one after another, all equally dismal.

Activity: Explaining an effect

Now you try the eight-step process on this extract and the question:

What impression does the writer give of the woman?

The extract follows on from the one on page 109:

> At the back of one of the houses a young woman was kneeling on the stones, poking a stick up the leaden waste-pipe which ran from the sink inside and which I suppose was blocked. I had time to see everything about her – her sacking apron, her clumsy clogs, her arms reddened by the cold. She had a round pale face, the usual exhausted face of the slum girl who is twenty-five and looks forty, thanks to miscarriages and drudgery; and it wore, for the second in which I saw it, the most desolate, hopeless expression I have ever seen.

From *The Road to Wigan Pier* by George Orwell

Offering an interpretation

Sometimes the explanation goes wider than just how the language works. You may, for example, want to explain:

- a moral or message
- a symbol
- a deeper meaning
- a theme
- an aspect that goes beyond the text, e.g. to the writer's life and times.

The question you are asking is: *What is this text really about?*

For example, this very short story is about a monkey – or is it?

The night of the monkey

The monkey came.

It smoked her fags. Ate her food. Threw up in the sink. Lost her shoes. Drank her booze. Stole her purse. Bought a kebab. Kidnapped some bloke. Reparked her car. Trashed her room. Swapped her brain for cottonwool.

Next day she swore – she'd never drink again.

by Claire Evans

Activity: Interpretation

The monkey is not real. What does it represent? Discuss this then turn to the end of the masterclass for the answer.

Talking about the deeper meaning

To offer an interpretation of a text, you need to warn the reader that you are going beyond what is actually in the text. Useful wordings:

- *The underlying message is that...*
- *The implication is that...*
- *This symbolises...*
- *The writer is suggesting that...*
- *At another level, the writer is saying that...*

Activity: Stories

Here are two more short stories. Write a sentence or two about each one, to draw out their meaning:

Jane had been taken for granted as a wife and a mother, until the lottery.

She left home, bought a yacht, and travelled the world, making many new men friends. Some demanded considerable financial support.

Eventually, penniless, she returned home.

'Have you been out?' asked the children, casually.

by Colin Keighley

'Don't you ever cry?' yelled the bully.

The boy remained silent.

'Empty your pockets, and I mean empty.'

The boy obliged.

'Hanky – ugh! Keep that. Chocolate, pen, notebook – ha you're a trainspotter. Seven pounds ten pence – what's in this bottle then?'

'Those are the tears I've cried,' replied the boy.

by Bett Wareing

>> Test it

Your test task is to explain how George Orwell recreates the sights and sounds of the night when he gathered with other soldiers to march to war:

> The train was due to leave at eight and it was about ten past eight when the harassed, sweating officers managed to marshal us in the barrack square. I remember vividly the torchlit scene – the uproar and excitement, the red flags flapping in the torchlight, the massed ranks of militia men and the shouting and the clatter of boots and tin pannikins, and then some political commissar standing beneath a huge rolling red banner and making us a speech. Once again there was the conquering-hero stuff – shouting and enthusiasm, red flags and red and black flags everywhere, friendly crowds thronging the pavement to have a look at us, women waving from the windows. How natural it all seemed then; how remote and improbable now!

From *Homage to Catalonia* by George Orwell

What you get marks for

Saying what the overall effect is in the first line	2 marks
Showing how Orwell uses images to recreate sights and sounds	2 marks
Showing how the sentences are shaped to recreate the sensations of being there	2 marks
Quoting words and phrases that have a particular effect	2 marks
Finishing with an explanation of how it all works	2 marks
Total	**10 marks**

ANSWERS

The night of the monkey

The monkey is a symbol of her alcoholism. Because she cannot remember her drunken behaviour, it feels as though she has been possessed or that someone else did it. The monkey is this imaginary drunkard.

20. Answers to big questions

In this masterclass you will learn how to:

- understand what you are being asked to do in 'big' examination questions
- plan an appropriate answer
- start and conclude.

Understanding the question

You need to understand three things about the question or title:

- what it is about generally
- what it is about specifically
- what it wants you to do.

Example

How important was American public opinion in ending the Vietnam war?

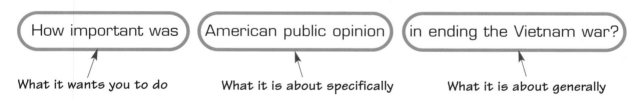

Activity: Analysing titles

Analyse these titles in the same way as the one above:

Analyse Macbeth's motives for killing Duncan.

Explore the moral arguments for and against human cloning.

Describe the effects of the monsoon in Asia.

Use the data spreadsheet to interpret the relationship between road accidents and traffic density, speed and type.

Explain how a pulley works.

Getting focused

The three most common reasons why people lose marks on big questions are:

1   They don't know the answer.

2   They write about the topic but not in the way they were asked to.

3   They write a brief correct answer but don't explain their thinking or 'working out'.

You will never be asked just to write about something. You will always be asked to write about it in a particular way or from a particular angle. The most important word in the question is the one which tells you what to do.

There are three main types of question:

1 'Say what you know' questions

These are the easiest questions because they are factual. The task is to present clearly what you know by listing or recounting the key points.

Key words:

- Describe
- Explain
- Define
- Give

To win extra marks:

- Illustrate each point with an example or quote
- Give detail
- Comment on the significance of things you describe
- Link the points

2 'Reorganise what you know' questions

These questions ask you to apply or rework what you know. They are harder because you have to structure your writing around the type of question. This means selecting relevant information and putting it in a useful order.

Key words:

- Discuss
- Explore
- Trace
- Compare
- Contrast
- Justify

To win extra marks:

- Pay extra attention to how you plan and structure the writing
- Use logical language
- Acknowledge other points of view

3 'Evaluate what you know' questions

These questions ask you to pass judgement and justify your answer.
They ask you to weigh up pros and cons and make a balanced review.

Key words:

- How far...?
- To what extent...?
- Why...?
- Evaluate
- Consider
- Review

To win extra marks:

- Acknowledge grey areas because the issues here are rarely 'black and white'
- Weigh each element separately
- Avoid glib or repetitious answers

Activity: Question types

Study these questions.

1 Explain the structure of the periodic table in chemistry.
2 What moral issues are raised by voluntary euthanasia (mercy killing)?
3 What factors led to the rise of fascism in Germany?
4 Compare William Wordsworth's poem *Daffodils* with his sister's diary entry on which it was based.
5 How effective is prison in preventing crime?
6 Describe the life cycle of a fruit fly.

For each one, discuss:

- what sort of question it is
- how you would structure an answer to it
- what kind of diagram or framework you would use to plan it.

Planning an answer

To gather ideas, use a diagram that suits the question. For example:

Compare William Wordsworth's poem *Daffodils* with his sister's diary entry on which it was based.

WILLIAM WORDSWORTH ESQ

	Dorothy's diary	William's poem
Similarities	Certain words used in both – he has lifted from Dorothy's diary Both written in first person	
Differences	Prose Other people were present	Poetry He is alone, 'I wandered lonely as a cloud'
Other points	She wrote the diary first	He didn't see the daffodils – he borrowed the idea from Dorothy's diary

Activity: Gathering ideas

This is a task to do in groups. Here is a grid for gathering ideas to answer the question: *How effective is prison in preventing crime?* Copy it and fill in as many points as you can think of. To start you off here are two points:

- When people are in prison, they can't commit crimes on the public.
- When people are in prison, they gang up with other criminals.

Very effective	Sometimes effective	Often ineffective	Very ineffective

Starting an answer

Your opening should:

- be quite brief
- unpack any difficulties or issues implied in the question
- suggest or summarise the overall answer
- move quickly to the first big point in the next paragraph.

Example: What moral issues are raised by voluntary euthanasia?

For religious people, voluntary euthanasia raises only one moral issue: is it right or wrong to take a life at all? They reject euthanasia because it is suicide and therefore against God's will. For others, euthanasia raises a host of questions about when it is justified and who should decide.

The most common form of euthanasia around the world is used for terminally ill patients who...

Concluding an answer

Your conclusion should:

- answer the question in summary
- be quite brief
- give a sense of balance and finality
- leave behind food for thought
- avoid a boring repetition of the opening.

Example: Closing the discussion about voluntary euthanasia

The moral issues are not, therefore, to be confused with the practical issues of how it is done and who does it. The real questions are about defining when life is no longer worth living, the rights of individuals to choose their own deaths, and the responsibilities of doctors, lawyers, families and the church in that decision.

Activity

Write the first and concluding paragraph of an answer to the question: *How effective is prison in preventing crime?*

Your test task is to:

1 Plan an answer to the following question (10 minutes).

2 Write the opening paragraph (10 minutes).

3 Write the concluding paragraph (10 minutes).

The question is:

Is a manned mission to Mars a giant step for mankind or a waste of money?

What you get marks for

Part 1

Planning in a suitable diagram or format	1 mark
Planning three to five main points to make	2 marks

Part 2

Writing a short, clear introduction	1 mark
Unpacking any difficulty or issues in the question	1 mark
Getting the reader's interest or attention	1 mark

Part 3

Answering the question	1 mark
Bringing a sense of balance and finality	1 mark
A strong, convincing conclusion	2 marks
Total	**10 marks**

21. Notes to the pupil

1. Have a plan you can hold in your head

Example 1: A piece of personal writing

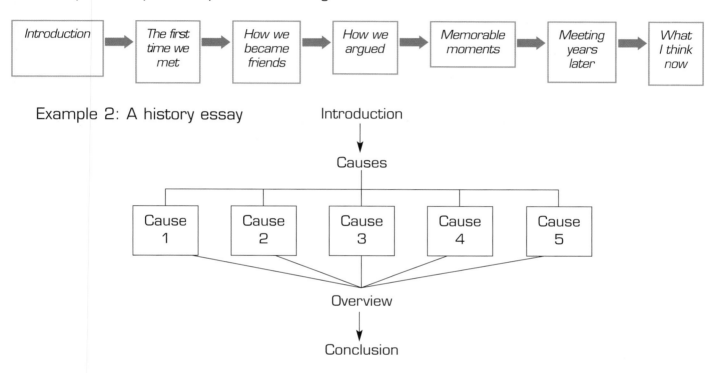

| Introduction | The first time we met | How we became friends | How we argued | Memorable moments | Meeting years later | What I think now |

Example 2: A history essay

Introduction

Causes

| Cause 1 | Cause 2 | Cause 3 | Cause 4 | Cause 5 |

Overview

Conclusion

2. Stuck for ideas?
Use a planning shape to get ideas flowing

For and against columns   **Star chart**

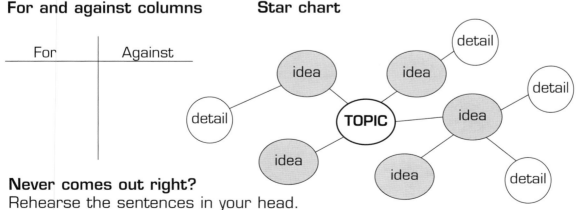

For	Against

Never comes out right?
Rehearse the sentences in your head.
If the sentence is too long to remember, at least know how it will end.
Consider breaking it up into two sentences.

3. Sounds flat? Vary the way you start your sentences

Try starting with an adverb:

> <u>Slowly</u> he begins to think there is something wrong.

Or an adjective:

> <u>Talented, beautiful</u> Emma realises she is out of luck at last.

Or with a verb:

> <u>Returning</u> home, she has a sense that every good thing in her life is over.

Or a preposition:

> <u>Beyond</u> the gate, something has stirred in the darkness.

4. Replace some dull verbs with powerful verbs

Example:

>   slithers   gliding
> The creature ~~draws~~ closer to the house, ~~moving~~ on a trail of sticky slime.

5. Replace some general nouns with strong specific nouns

Example:

>   porch   slick
> The creature slithers closer to the ~~house~~, gliding on a ~~trail~~ of
>   mucus
> sticky ~~slime~~.

6. Looks untidy? Line up and leave space

Even the worst handwriting looks better if you stick to the margin and leave space round each answer.

Before:

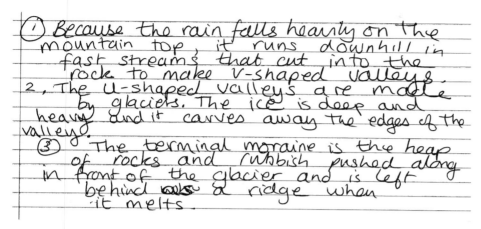

After:

1. Because the rain falls heavily on the mountain, it runs downhill in fast streams that cut into the rock to make V-shaped valleys.

2. The U-shaped valleys are made by glaciers. The ice is deep and heavy, and carves away the edges of the valley.

3. The terminal moraine is the heap of rocks and rubbish pushed along at the front of the glacier and is left behind as a ridge when it melts.

7. Horrible handwriting? Tidy up with six simple rules

1 Slope it all in the same direction (pencil in lines if you have to).

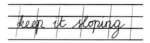

2 Make all the tails the same.

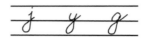

3 Keep it on the line.

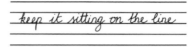

4 Change to a fountain pen with a thick nib.

5 Keep the small letters all the same height.

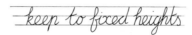

6 Change your worst letters one at a time for a week at a time.

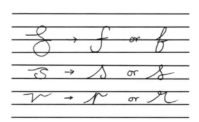

Try sticking to rule 1 for the first week.

Try sticking to rules 1 and 2 for the second week.

Try sticking to rules 1, 2 and 3 for the third week.

And so on...

8. Spelling's a nightmare? Learn the top 5 rules, 50 common words and top tips for learning

1 Plurals

Most plurals just add S.

Some words add ES because they end in a hissing, shushing or buzzing sound. The ES creates an extra syllable.

marsh – marshes   fizz – fizzes

2 Doubling

Why one T in *writing* but two in *written*?

Why one N in *dining* but two in *dinner*?

Here's the trick: listen to the vowel just before it.

* If it's a long vowel (one that says its own name), use a single letter.
* If it's a short vowel, use double letters.

3 Adding prefixes

Just add prefixes. They never change the word.

dis + appear = disappear   dis + satisfied = dissatisfied

4 Adding suffixes

Most suffixes can just be added, but watch out for:

Words ending in consonant + Y, e.g. *pity*

* Change Y to I if you add a suffix, e.g. pitiful, pitied, pitiless.
* But avoid two vowels together, e.g. pitying, not pitiing.

Words ending in consonant + E

* Keep the E in most cases.
* But avoid two vowels together, e.g. boring, not boreing.

5 Take care when two vowels sit together

IE – most common, e.g. thief.

EI – after C, e.g. receive or when it sounds like A, e.g. vein.

A–E – the most common long A spelling, e.g. stale.

O–E – the most common long O spelling, e.g. note.

OW – usually at the end of words, e.g. cow.

OU – usually at the start or in the middle of words, e.g. out, mouse.

Fifty words that are often misspelt

Learn them.

1. alcohol
2. although
3. autumn
4. beautiful
5. because
6. beginning
7. believe
8. business
9. chocolate
10. daughter
11. definitely
12. design
13. environment
14. February
15. forty
16. guard
17. happened

18. health
19. height
20. imaginary
21. interest
22. knowledge
23. listening
24. marriage
25. material
26. necessary
27. parallel
28. people
29. permanent
30. physical
31. possession
32. process
33. receive
34. remember

35. research
36. Saturday
37. secondary
38. separate
39. sincerely
40. soldier
41. stomach
42. straight
43. strength
44. success
45. surprise
46. technology
47. tomorrow
48. Wednesday
49. weight
50. women

Ten ways to remember spellings

- Break it into sounds (a-l-c-o-h-o-l).
- Break it into syllables (re-mem-ber).
- Break it into sections (re + search).
- Use a memory trick (ne**cess**ary – one **c**ollar, two **s**leeves).
- Think of a word in the same family (e.g. strong – strength).
- Say it as it sounds (Wed-nes-day).
- Words within words (heal in health).
- Refer to etymology (Saturday = Saturn Day).
- Link to word families and learn a key word (height, weight, freight, eight).
- Learning it by looking.

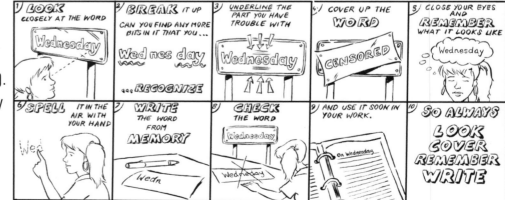

Soundalikes

These words are often mixed up. Here's a way to remember which is which:

Confusions	How to remember which is which
affect/effect	• *Affect* is what you do (verb) • *Effect* is the result (noun) • If you forget, use *effect* – it's used more often
allowed/aloud	• *Allowed* ends in ED because it's a past tense verb: *allow/allowed* • The word *loud* within *aloud* is a clue
bought/brought	• Say it slowly to hear the R • Link *brought* to *bring*
choose/chose	• OO says OO • Remember the double letter by remembering *Choose cheese*
cloth/clothe	• The E at the end makes the O long; compare *not/note*
our/are	• *Our* can be linked to the other pronoun *your*
practice/practise	• C is the noun • S is the verb • Easy-to-hear comparisons: *advice/advise* and *device/devise*
quiet/quite	• Say it slowly to hear the E before the T – it makes an extra syllable
threw/through	Learn: • I *knew* who *threw* it • *Through* the *rough* field
their/there	• Learn *their heirlooms* as a way of remembering which one means 'belonging to them' • Link *there* to *here* and *where*
to/too/two	• *To* is the most common one if you are not sure • The double O in *too* reminds you it means *too* many • *Two* links to *twice*

These are separate words:

• a lot of   • thank you

22. Notes to parents and helpers

This chapter contains advice about how to help a young person to compose a piece of writing, and then offers ideas for encouraging better writing.

Helping growing writers

Do you remember when they were very little, and you read a bedtime story? Or when they went to primary school how they brought home books and you listened to them read? The problem with writing is that no one ever writes a story at bedtime or listens to their children writing. It's not obvious how to share writing.

It's the same at school. There's plenty of help to get going, and there's marking afterwards, but something is missing in the middle – help at the time of writing.

This is how to do it.

Getting started

Sit with them before they start and get them to tell you what they have to do. Don't cross-question them: it makes them clam up.

Make sure they know these things before they start:

- the title or question
- the point of doing it
- how long it should be
- what style it should be.

And if you're lucky:

- what the teacher said about the task (if it is a school task)
- the mark scheme (sometimes pasted in the exercise book)
- if they're allowed to word-process it.

Ask them to tell you the main things they need to say and what order to say them. This will be the writing plan. You write it. This is going to be harder than you think; it's surprising how often older children start writing without having a map of the writing in their heads. Ask clarifying questions as you go and finish by repeating back the order of points as you understand them.

If you or they find this really difficult, you may need to drop back to an earlier stage of gathering ideas.

Ask them how they're going to start. Some people find this incredibly challenging and they freeze up. If so, leave a space and you can go back to it later. Instead, start with the first proper point.

The process of writing

Ask them to tell you in their own words how they will express the first point or paragraph. If they seem pretty confident about it, get them to write it down and watch what they do.

Hold back on the criticism. It is really tempting to jump in at the first spelling error or offbeat expression and put it right. But don't do it. They will hate it and never want to write with you again. Also, don't do all the work for them even if it makes you feel good, because the idea is to help them to do it for themselves. On the other hand, approve of anything good such as:

- a well-chosen word
- a well-expressed idea
- a good opening line
- spelling a tricky word
- use of links, e.g. conversely, thus, although
- mature expression.

At the end of each paragraph, sum up what is good about the paragraph and allow yourself one other comment. Don't express it as a negative, and avoid interrogation. Make plain and obvious points and speak on your own behalf as a reader. For example:

- I think you've left a letter out of this word.
- I'm not clear what you're saying at the end here.
- So this is everything you want to say on this topic?
- This expression sounds odd to me.
- Check the punctuation in the middle there.
- I think you've missed a comma.

The idea is to alert them to the problem but let them sort it out. Don't abandon them, though. Allow a few moments for them to act. If they're plainly stuck, ask them to tell you what they're thinking.

- Tell me what you're thinking.
- What will you do?
- Tell me how you'll change it.
- Any ideas?

Now you can help by refining their ideas rather than substituting your own. Do this quickly. No slogging.

Getting on with it

Now let them get on with the writing for a while. It's too much to write the whole thing with them. Ask them to call you over when they get to a tricky bit.

The kitchen table is a pretty good place for writing because they can sit at it to write whilst you potter in the background. Stay around, avoid chatting and don't hover. And especially don't go sniping for errors.

When they're done, ask them to read the whole thing to you. This is for them more than it is for you. They will sense the effect of what they've written. Don't interrupt. Make at least two positive comments. Be specific – 'That's okay' won't do; you have to say what is okay, for example: 'The opening is strong, and you make a good point about newspapers.'

Depending on their mood, ask if they want you to proofread it for them or pick up on one point that was unclear during the reading.

Checking

If you proofread, indicate where the problems lie but don't correct it for them. Instead, give them a prompt:

- I think you've got a letter too many in that word – do you know which one it is?
- You've mixed up *there* and *their* – how do you know which is which?
- There's a full stop missing on this line – where should it go?
- There's a punctuation error on this line – can you see it?

Your main aim here is to teach them the right way to do it. But if they are struggling, don't slog. Tell them the general rule and how to correct the mistake. Let them correct it. Ideally, make a note that they can keep as an aide-mémoire. A sheet in a ring binder is good, or a sheet blu-tacked to the kitchen wall.

Showing an interest

You may find over the next day or so that the topic about which you were writing comes into your mind, or something will come up that reminds you of it. Mention it to your offspring: it's good that they know you found it interesting, that you looked beyond the spelling and punctuation. It says that writing has meaning.

Other things you can do to help

1. Help with written homework (but don't do it for them)

Make only constructive comments and ask questions such as these:

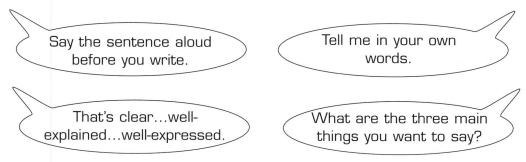

Say the sentence aloud before you write.

Tell me in your own words.

That's clear...well-explained...well-expressed.

What are the three main things you want to say?

2. Give gifts that encourage writing

e.g. diary, stationery, fountain pen, stamps, card-making software.

3. Play games that improve spelling

e.g. Scrabble, Boggle, Lexicon, crosswords, word searches.

4. Buy an easy-to-read dictionary and a thesaurus

Look for clear print, boldfaced words and simple explanations.

5. Put up spelling checklists

Put them in places where they will be seen often, e.g. bedside, toilet door.

6. Ask them to do writing for the family

e.g. shopping lists, packing lists, postcards, emails.

7. Encourage them to read more

Take them to visit libraries and bookshops. Read their set texts. Point out interesting articles. Subscribe to a magazine. Buy book tokens.

8. If they use a word processor, advise them how to use the facilities for checking, editing and presentation

The **checking** facilities include – the spellchecker, thesaurus, grammar check, word count and the track changes facilities. Most software has a setting that underlines spelling errors and grammatical issues as you type.

The **editing** facilities include cut, copy and paste.

The **presentation** facilities are usually listed under a drop-down format menu. It includes font size and shape, borders, shading, bullet styles, paragraph styles, etc. Many programmes now offer help with common layouts such as letters.

Some things that don't work

Forcing them to write

It's not really about writing more; it's about knowing how to compose. Practice is important at a certain stage, but you can end up recycling mistakes. If you want to write with your son or daughter, keep it to a few sentences and focus on expression.

Telling them what to write

If you tell them what to write, you'll get good at it but they will become dependent on you. The main thing is to help them do it for themselves. Ask helpful questions or make broad suggestions.

Expecting perfection

Stick to one or two points of help, and do it little and often. It's demoralising for them if you always expect perfection. Luckily, you have your children for life, so you can afford to take your time.

23. Notes to the teacher

Characteristics of writers at Level 5

The writers at whom this book is targeted are already reasonably competent in organising and expressing themselves. In terms of the National Curriculum, Level 5 writers are described thus:

> **Pupils' writing is varied and interesting, conveying meaning clearly in a range of forms for different readers, using a more formal style where appropriate. Vocabulary choices are imaginative and words are used precisely. Simple and complex sentences are organised into paragraphs. Words with complex regular patterns are usually spelt correctly. A range of punctuation, including commas, apostrophes and inverted commas, is usually used accurately. Handwriting is joined, clear and fluent and, where appropriate, is adapted to a range of tasks.**

It is a formidable level descriptor characterised by writing which is 'varied', 'interesting', 'clear', 'imaginative' and 'precise', but curiously deflated by cautious descriptions at the end of it which refer to basic skills which are only 'usually' right. In reality, we can say that pupils at Level 5 are pretty good writers already, but they will have uneven success attaining the clarity and precision claimed in the descriptor. The expression and organisation of sophisticated ideas remains a key task.

Many Level 5 writers have got where they are by reading a lot. They are sure-footed with familiar styles and tasks, because they know how they should sound and look, and they can also make a business-like sentence. But very often they are leaning on the familiar, confident with the commonplace, and (as is the case with reading), in danger of sitting on a plateau hoping that experience alone will raise their game.

And that slight hesitation in the descriptor about the accuracy of basic skills is justified. It is very common to find writers at Level 5 who have come through the system with outstanding weaknesses in spelling and punctuation. It is hardly likely that these weaknesses will go away at this stage as if by magic; they need direct attention. As the content and organisation of their work progresses, those residual weaknesses show up even more.

Moving from Level 5 to Level 6

The move from Level 5 to Level 6 is the one from competence to control. Looking ahead, the Level 6 writer that will emerge is described in the National Curriculum thus:

> **Pupils' writing often engages and sustains the reader's interest, showing some adaptation of style and register to different forms, including using an impersonal style, where appropriate. Pupils use a range of sentence structures and varied vocabulary to create effects. Spelling is generally accurate, including that of irregular words. Handwriting is neat and legible. A range of punctuation is usually used correctly to clarify meaning, and ideas are organised into paragraphs.**

This terrifying level descriptor leaves behind it a terrible dread of what Level 7 might contain – what on earth is there left to do? There are many professional writers who have not attained Level 6 if this is what it is. The danger for teachers is that we work out Level 6 by negative marking, seeking the mistakes and inelegances that tell us that a piece of writing is *not* a Level 6. It paints an image of a writer whose errors are gradually dying away (how?) and at the same time developing ever more dazzling skills for impressing the reader. A glance at Level 7 reveals that the same pupil has acquired the gloss of self-assurance: 'confident', 'developed', 'coherent'. Teaching Level 6 has to be more than just sweeping up spelling and commas. We can't give up on progression before GCSE has even started.

So what are the hallmarks of a pupil who is reaching up above the level of competence described in Level 5?

Firstly, they are securing a grip on complex sentence structures so that their writing can carry more sophisticated meanings. As writers strive to create more elaborate sentences, they find that the demands on punctuation increase. If writers can't use the comma and the semicolon to partition clauses, then there are severe constraints on their ability to express complex ideas. One has to be confident with internal sentence punctuation to get Level 6. It is not unusual to find pupils stuck at Level 5 because they employ avoidance strategies, keeping to short sentences and unambitious vocabulary because they are afraid of making mistakes with complex spelling and sentence grammar. So one clear task is to help them to secure their control over expression at sentence level. This issue is addressed in Section B of this book.

Secondly, they are moving beyond the sound of their own voices to the repertoire of more adult voices that speak in standard English, that discuss, analyse, criticise, compare, hypothesise and so on. These are higher order text types, more challenging than information, instruction, explanation and recount which are now well-established in Years 4–7 as a result of the National Literacy Strategy. These new text types contain more variables, more subtle transitions between points, and a greater command of materials and voice. It is the difference between expressing one's own opinion and presenting a range of opinions; between giving information and offering advice; between response to literature and critical analysis; between brainstorming ideas and speculating with them. So another task is to develop a new range of adaptable adult voices. This is addressed in Section C.

Thirdly, as their powers of expression improve, pupils must begin to manipulate the organisation of text. In narrative, this means managing perspective and narrative devices. In non-fiction it means gathering and synthesising ideas into coherent writing. Much of this organising takes place at the planning stage. The Level 6 writer has a conscious writing strategy that is more than a paragraph plan or a running order: it is a strategy for how to tell. These issues are addressed in Section A for narrative and Section D for non-narrative.

Fourthly, and not unconnected with the three points above, is getting ready for tests. One section – Section E – is dedicated to the kind of writing that is demanded in the KS3 tests, though the skills of analysis and quotation are relevant beyond the English curriculum. The four masterclasses in Section E are also relevant to other tests in KS2 and GCSE.

Using this book

This book is arranged in masterclasses which will fill two or maybe three lessons depending on the length of your lessons. The masterclasses also break down quite easily so they can be spread in shorter blocks of around 20 minutes. The intention is to move at a cracking pace, and the focus is on quality rather than quantity.

All the masterclasses are about the art of expression. Most of them concentrate on paragraphs and sentences, and some of them on planning at text level. The main focus throughout is on how ideas are formulated and clarified in writing because this has proved the most difficult aspect of writing to teach in large classes, and it is clear enough that retrospective marking is not enough to get pupils writing in lucid, sharp prose.

The masterclasses address the issue of composition itself, and are meant to aid teaching at that shaping moment when pupils attempt to put their thoughts into words. The book is tightly structured to guide pupils through the process of composition, leaving you free to work at close quarters with one or more pupils.

To add value, there are two things you can do:

- For key activities, demonstrate on the board how you would tackle them, composing on the spot and thinking aloud about what you are doing – why you choose particular words, why you delete particular words, what you are considering, how you rate it, what sounds wrong, what needs changing, what effect you're trying for and so on. The purpose of this is to give pupils an insight into the dynamics of composition.
- Take turns to sit by pupils who seem to struggle with writing and watch them compose. Ask them to talk aloud as you have just done, to reveal to you the process they are going through. Your purpose is to unblock the process by giving them compositional strategies that work.

The masterclasses can be used flexibly, for example:

- mini-units positioned between longer units of work
- group study units for up to six pupils at Level 5
- guided writing groups
- a substantial unit of work on *Improving expression*.

Because you are expecting pupils to improve and revise their expression, they should be doing a lot of amendments. A word processor is an ideal tool. To retain their amendments so that you can review their drafting, show them how to use the track changes facility which will record amendments but can also remove them at the touch of a button revealing the clean copy.

Also in this book are *Notes for parents and helpers* on page 128 and *Notes to the pupil* on page 121. As a minimum you should set these as reading homeworks. Even better, use them to set an agenda for a parents' evening on writing. As you work through the ideas and advice, get parents to try sample activities such as spotting words within words in a list of key spellings. Many schools offer evenings on reading, but writing recruits just as well. If you have a video camera, they will be impressed to see a video showing a teacher working alongside a pupil. Sell them dictionaries, spelling games, writing materials and books. Parents and helpers are a valuable resource.